W0082207

I Found It at the Movies:

An Anthology of Film Poems

ESSENTIAL ANTHOLOGIES SERIES 6

Canada Council for the Arts

Conseil des Arts du Canada

Guernica Editions Inc. acknowledges the support of the
Canada Council for the Arts and the Ontario Arts Council.
The Ontario Arts Council is an agency of the Government of Ontario.

We acknowledge the financial support of the Government of Canada
through the Canada Book Fund (CBF) for our publishing activities.

I Found It at the Movies:

An Anthology of Film Poems

Edited by

Ruth Roach Pierson

GUERNICA

TORONTO—BUFFALO—LANCASTER (U.K.)

2014

AURORA PUBLIC LIBRARY

Copyright © 2014, the Editor, the Authors and Guernica Editions Inc.
All rights reserved. The use of any part of this publication,
reproduced, transmitted in any form or by any means, electronic,
mechanical, photocopying, recording or otherwise stored in a
retrieval system, without the prior consent of the publisher is an
infringement of the copyright law.

Ruth Roach Pierson, editor
Michael Mirolla, general editor
Interior design by Jill Ronsley
Guernica Editions Inc.
P.O. Box 76080, Abbey Market, Oakville, (ON), Canada L6M 3H5
2250 Military Road, Tonawanda, N.Y. 14150-6000 U.S.A.

Distributors:
University of Toronto Press Distribution,
5201 Dufferin Street, Toronto (ON), Canada M3H 5T8
Gazelle Book Services, White Cross Mills, High Town, Lancaster LA1 4XS U.K.

First edition.
Printed in Canada.

Legal Deposit—Third Quarter
Library of Congress Catalog Card Number: 2013954689
Library and Archives Canada Cataloguing in Publication

I found it at the movies / edited by Ruth Roach Pierson.

(Essential anthologies series ; 6)
Issued in print and electronic formats.
ISBN 978-1-55071-897-3 (pbk.).–ISBN 978-1-55071-898-0 (epub).–
ISBN 978-1-55071-899-7 (mobi)

1. Motion pictures–Poetry. 2. Canadian poetry (English)–20th
century. 3. Canadian poetry (English)–21st century. 4. American
poetry–20th century. 5. American poetry–21st century. I. Pierson,
Ruth Roach, 1938-, editor of compilation II. Series: Essential
anthologies series (Toronto, Ont.) ; 6

PS8287.M68I36 2014   C811'.54080357   C2013-907719-7
                                                C2013-907720-0

CONTENTS

STARS, STUNTMEN AND A CAMEO APPEARANCE   77

DIRECTORS, CHOREOGRAPHERS, CRITICS, AND WANNABES

SCARY MOVIES, THRILLERS, HORROR FLICKS AND FILM NOIR

INTRODUCTION

INCONTESTABLY MOVIES PLAY an important role in the lives of most of us, poets included. Movies, all kinds of movies, are part of our common experience. For some of us, it's occasionally difficult to draw a sharp line between movie and life. On a car trip through the Canadian Shield some years ago, a friend of mine commented on how paintings by members of the Group of Seven organized her view of the landscape. I think the same could be said of the impact movies can have on our perceptions. One might say movies provide a prism through which we view our lives. In "Emerald City Blues," Phoebe Tsang sees Hong Kong through remembered images from "The Wizard of Oz." Barry Dempster, on his ramble through a Simcoe County forest, is visited by scenes of Russian birches from Tarkovsky's *Ivan's Childhood*. If asked: "Which would you choose: movies or life?", how many of us might answer, on some occasion or other: "Movies!" In the 1970s, after viewing, during a long Victoria Day Weekend, twenty-two films in four days at the Annual Meeting of the Canadian Federation of Film Societies, I looked out the window of the train on which I was travelling and, thinking the take of passing landscape was going on far too long, caught myself just before crying out: "Cut!"

And who among us have never seen ourselves or wished to see ourselves reflected in characters played by actors with whom we identify? I confess that, through much of the 1960s, I wanted desperately to become Jeanne Moreau. Don McKay writes: "Movies have been sent to us to make up for the bathroom mirror." In his poem "Glenn Gould watches *Thirty-two Short Films about Glenn Gould*," Steve McOrmond contends:

Anyone should have the right to pay
admission and watch their lives flickering
forty feet in the air while they eat their popcorn.

But depending on our social location, we can also experience Hollywood superstars as icons of menace. John Wayne stands in for a violent father in Jim Smith's "John" and, in David Groulx's "Instruments of Oz or Paranoid Indian," for the contemptuous and often hate-filled depiction of native people in westerns.

Movies become inextricably woven into our life experiences and thereby into the warp and weft of our memories. Steven Heighton captures this in his poem *"2001, An Elegy"* which begins with his childhood recollection of watching Kubrick's 1968 movie in his mother's company and goes on to merge into his memory of her death in 2001. In the poems of a number of poets, the experience of visiting a particular movie theatre or drive-in when a child or teenager is remembered as a turning point in their lives.

Seeing Ingmar Bergman's *The Magician* in 1958 in the company of a couple of sorority sisters and our dates became a turning point for me. Most remarkable was the fact that this group of bobby soxers and frat boys couldn't stop talking about the film after we left the movie theatre and drove to the local drive-in for hamburgers and root beer floats. We had been mesmerized by a film about a mesmerist and were puzzled about what it meant. This had never happened before, not after seeing *Some Like It Hot* or *Seven Brides for Seven Brothers* or *Giant* or *Funny Face*, not even after seeing *The Bridge on the River Kwai*. It was a revelation that triggered a conversion experience—from casual moviegoer to enthusiast, from local movie theatre to art house, from picture palace to repertory cinema, and from movies as mere entertainment to film as art form, director as magician. I became a person who might have declared like the narrator in Todd Swift's poem "Sight and Sound":

I read of films to know which films to see.
I rarely, if ever, refer to them as movies.

It took years of reading Pauline Kael's hard-headed, no-holds-barred, inspired and impassioned movie reviews in *The New Yorker* with their ardent championing of the great Hollywood movies (while despising the effect of blockbusters and action films on the industry) for me to give up my foreign film snobbery and embrace the greatness of tinsel town's contribution to cinema. For this reason alone, I was thrilled when David Donnell suggested *I Found It At the Movies* as the title to this anthology.*

It was Sue MacLeod who came up with the idea for the anthology—after hearing me read "After Life" at my 2011 book launch of *Contrary*. Even though I name that movie within the body of the poem and use its title for the poem's, I had never thought of "After Life" as a "movie poem," presumably because the movie had not been the poem's trigger. But I leapt at Sue's idea, having written many other poems for which a particular movie or experience of movie-going had served as impulse. And I suspected that would be true of many other poets.

This suspicion was borne out by the many hundreds of poems submitted in response to the general call for submissions and the dozens more uncovered by perusing poetry collections and reaching out to poets suspected of harbouring movie poems. The result is an anthology that contains something for everyone. The variety of movies referenced is considerable—ranging from silent films (Peter Richardson's reference to Harold Lloyd's hanging from a clock face in the 1923 silent film *Safety Last*) to a 2012 comedy (Patria Rivera on *Best Exotic Marigold Hotel*), from a 1930 USSR classic (Sandra Stechisen's "*Zemlya*: Dovzhenko's *Earth* as seen from a Canadian Cinema") to a 1996 Canadian movie (Carleton Wilson's "On Once Again Watching Bruce McDonald's *Hard Core Logo*"), from post-World War Two Italian neo-realism (Jacqueline Bourque on Vittorio De Sica's 1948 *Bicycle Thieves*) to the French New Wave cinema of the 1960's (Darren Bifford on Jean-Luc Godard's *Breathless*). The range extends from vampire films (Emily Schultz and Vanessa Moeller on *Nosferatu*) to monster flicks (Sachiko Murakami on *Godzilla*) and includes love poems to famous actors (Karen Solie's to Robert Mitchum, Michael Kenyon's to Toshiro Mifune), tributes to directors (Lillian Necakov's to Jean Vigo) as well as to choreographers (Craig Poile's to Fred Astaire's collaborator Hermes Pan), along with Sharon McCartney's send-up of the two cartoon characters Wile E. Coyote and Road Runner. The collection as a whole also demonstrates how film serves as a source of metaphor and compositional structure, exemplifying the symbiotic relationship between the two art forms: poetic cinema, cinematic poetry.

Sprinkled through the contributions to this anthology are many cinematic terms for which I have not provided a glossary, confident readers are familiar with almost all of them (the major exception being "cukaloris" for which Jason Guriel gives a definition in the epigraph accompanying his poem bearing that title). An appendix lists the movies/films referenced in the anthology, providing title, country of origin, date of release, and name(s) of director(s). The decision not to name the films' scriptwriters or the actors in starring roles reveals me to be more of a supporter of auteur theory than I thought I was.

Most importantly, the hope of all of those who have contributed to bringing this anthology to fruition is that the anthology will find readers who enjoy reading poems about movies as much as seeing the movies themselves.

—Ruth Roach Pierson

* The title plays, of course, on Pauline Kael's first collection of her *New Yorker* movie reviews, *I Lost It at the Movies* (Boston: Little, Brown, 1965). When asked in later years by an interviewer what it was she had "lost," Kael answered: "There are so many kinds of innocence to be lost at the movies."—Hollis Alpert, "Raising Kael," *The Saturday Review*, 24 April 1971 (Wikipedia article accessed August 1, 2012)

THE EXPERIENCE

STILLNESS

Maleea Acker

The stillness in every season is extreme for a moment,
then soon, gone,
replaced, indistinctly, by continuation.
When the cicadas begin,
the junco is a fugitive rustle in the leaves, now moving,
now waiting.
We find things altering; a mirage of warmth or cold
marks the midpoint, a small centre of spinning, a slow freeze—
like the sea scene in *The Four Hundred Blows*, when Antoine arrives
at the expanse of the wave
   and is drawn in.
Now then, I said, I go to meet that which I liken to.
        Always, the entry
and then the dreaming in. Then.
We do not remember exactly what follows:
dailiness goes on unmarked
as the edges of a doorway or a mirror.
It is the centre that interests, so this we recall.
The cicadas stop, begin again, then end.

I wish I could promise a concern
that would remain. That I might promise an attention
which gave its word not to wander, not to lull. There,
the rustle of the wing, the moulted feathers dislodging,
the flight across the terrace; there,
the song stitching the portal through which all of it comes;
there, the entry, watery, dark, flowing,
and we are in and it has flown.

Saturday Matinee

Brenda Sciberras

We walk down Main up to Logan
my hand in his colossal palm.

My father comforts
me with just his smile.

Big brother walks on ahead
denying any need. He's eleven.

We enter the Starland vestibule.
My father pulls change from his pocket,

a buck and a half for the three tickets, two
bits each for my brother and me. A bargain

for this Saturday matinee, a double feature.
King Kong and the Son of Kong.

The theatre's large paint peeled doors creak
open to a sculpted ceiling, faded and frayed carpet.

Maroon threadbare seats give off
a musty odour, a strange sour smell.

The popcorn has an old taste and the Nibs aren't soft.
We sit, backs against the wall, my father

in the middle, not so we don't fight, he says,
but so he can guard us with his watchful eyes.

I'm not sure who he is watching or why
but I sense that he should.

Lights dim. The curtain rises.
The overture begins.

A Comedy of (T)Errors, Or, Why I Hardly Ever Go to the Movies

Maureen Scott Harris

It wasn't yet the 1950s—or only just. The three of us
were loaded into the backseat in our pyjamas.
I was no older than 5, or maybe 6, and the car
was the first we'd ever had, a Hillman Minx—
or was it Minks, and how did we all fit inside?
I can almost see the pattern on my brother's legs,
small animals, dogs I think, or maybe pigs,
printed on blue flannel. We were off to the Pembina
Drive-in. If we stopped dawdling we'd get there
in time to play on the swings at the foot
of the looming screen, bigger than our house, blank
and innocent and quiet in daylight, but when the sky
began to darken the air pulsed and a giant
popping machine threatened to bury us in popcorn.

Our squabbles over spilled crackerjack and who
got to sit where rose over the tinny sounds from
the speaker that hung in the car, its curled cord
swaying in the prairie wind but still anchoring us.
During the previews my sister, a baby with a curl
on top of her head, crawled into the front seat
and fell asleep on our mother's lap. Now my brother
and I had some room but we could hardly see
past our parents' heads, and wriggled and bumped,
complaining 'til the newsreel's marching music ended
and cartoons made us laugh. When the round bulk
of Abbott and skinny-stick Costello flashed onto
the screen we squealed and bounced, ready for fun.

They were our favourites in the movies we'd seen
at the church—or was it at the Garry Theatre?
Real darkness settled around the screen's glow.
A throbbing full moon appeared and Abbott's arm—
or was it Costello's?—reached across that enormous
screen and began to grow fur. I screamed and screamed.
My father threatened we'd leave right now, my brother
howled that I always got what I wanted, and my mother
said, *stop that racket this minute, put your head
down on the seat.* Still wailing I slumped
to the floor and whimpered myself to sleep.

That's why I don't like the movies. They pretend
to be one thing and then become something else
and you never know what's what. I've searched
for that image of the ominous moon shining down
while a human arm slowly turns into a wolf's furred leg.
I can't find it. I'm sure the film was *Abbott and Costello
Meet the Werewolf.* I've found them meeting Frankenstein,
Dracula, The Mummy, Doctor Jekyll and Mr. Hyde,
Captain Kidd, The Invisible Man, The Killer, and
the Keystone Cops, but not the werewolf. It appears
there is no such movie ... perhaps none of this happened at all ...

NEW YEAR'S DAY, 1960

Maureen Hynes

The cousins set out in a line, down the middle
of the snow-packed street—a dozen of us
in our various heights, led by our tall uncle, a former priest.
Above us, the gleaming is miraculous: every finger
of every branch shines within a translucent glove,
nearly dazzling us silent. But what holds all this
in place, the deep snow and aching cold
and the girl cousins in our brown galoshes and ribbed lisle stockings
crunching down the street is the sky's blue—a field
of brightness so intense that we can only
squint our way forward into an afternoon of darkness,
heat and noise: four hours
of Ben-Hur in wide-screen Technicolor
and thundering charioteer sound.

BELLE DE JOUR

Rishma Dunlop

Dancing after school at Carole Bryan's house,
high on milk cartons in our white go-go boots
with zips up the back, we are Solid Gold Dancers
shaking and shimmying in fishnets and hot pants.

At slumber parties in our baby doll nighties,
nursing bottles of coke, we watch the *Ed Sullivan
Show*—Mick doing his bump and grind in Ed's
censored version of "Let's Spend the Night Together."

We watch old movies, Deneuve,
as Severine, the bored housewife, batting
false eyelashes above a white push-up bra,
having sex with strangers,

and Eva Marie Saint, as Edie,
dropping her small white dress glove
which Brando, as Terry, picks up
and pulls onto his brute boxer's paw.

At dawn, we strut through the house, Motown divas,
we perfect the gestures, hands cupping our hair,
up to our elbows in white evening gloves,
vamping to "Stop in the Name of Love."

DRIVE-IN, 1969

Deborah-Anne Tunney

watching the movie so many years later, this is what I think: one
night in the summer of my 17th year, at a drive-in with Margo and
Darlene and Jimmy, the air becoming thick silk, cool on my bare
arms as the sun went down and we were sitting in Jimmy's car, our
feet on the dashboard, on the chair backs, and this movie played
on the screen. It was like a TV being on in a living room, everyone
spoke over it, threw popcorn at each other, laughed and shouted
to friends who walked by, as we spun out the long, hilarious spool
of our teenage selves. But there was also something like ghosts
in the air, something coming, our adult versions perhaps, like
the birds that swooped down on the serene seaside town, and on
this night, before the hours in classrooms, in libraries, on buses
on the way to work, before the new people we would become:
here we were, our dusty feet, chipped polish like exotic scales, the
concession stand with its sticky floor under our flip flops, so real,
so full of smells and music, *the byrds, dylan, the rolling stones*, that
we did not notice our fate playing out in that living room with its
piano, its portrait of dead parents, the fireplace just before the
brimming glitter of wings.

14

SHORT FAT FLICKS

Don McKay

1. *He rides into town*

already perfect, already filled with nothing. His music is a hawk
scream which has been crossed with machine, perhaps eternity's
lathe, and fashioned into a horse. His hatbrim is horizon. It is
all over. Only the unspeakable trauma which erased his name
concerns him. Now it concerns the townsfolk as they scuttle,
gutless, behind shopfronts. Two minutes ago their houses were
three-dimensional and contained kitchens, not to mention
closets. Now the houses, the general store, livery, and sheriff's
office are so obviously props that the townsfolk have stopped
believing in them before the curtains twitch back into place. Now
they are cover awaiting shootout, and the townsfolk are extras
waiting to fall, aaargh, from their roofs, and crash, spratinkle
tinkle tinkle, through their windows. He rides into town from
another genre, from the black star that sucks the depth from
everything, a soundless bell tolling. *You should have changed your
life*, it says, *done, done, done*. Doesn't even consider that you fixed
up the den and took that night class in creative writing.

2. *Their eyes meet*

ah, and there is a satisfying drag on the sprockets, as though the
celluloid were suddenly too heavy to turn, as though the projector
were sleepy. One violin has been stricken and starts, legato,
a drugged smoke alarm, to troll the theme, which the camera
catches, tracking left (always left) to take in a quiver of lips. Close-
up, close-up, two-shot, their four eyes have begun to unbutton
and bud, the strings now ahum, vibrato, zoom zoom zoom they
shed the depth of field. Who needs it? The darkness is inhabited,

the popcorn is buttered. Their lips approach like shy cats. Her
eyes have decided to skinny-dip in his and his in hers: one more
micro zoom and they dive, leaving the rest of their faces behind to
nuzzle and rub, attempting to smudge the irregular line between
them. And the eyes? Are swimming with us, dolphins, in the
darkness, which is rich and viscous, the lake of tears we've been
waiting for.

3. *We take our seats*

and settle into our bodies, waiting for the lights to dim so we can
feel ourselves falling, this is the best part, feel ourselves falling
into a safer kind of sleep, an elaborate parkland of carefully pre-
pared surprises. As the curtains begin to part, *lingerie*, we can
see through them to the screen, which has begun to flicker into
being. Will the plot matter? Of course not. Movies have been sent
to us to make up for the bathroom mirror, with its rigid notion of
representation, and the family, with its chain-link semantic net.
Here we feel ideas wriggle into costume and images reach toward
us out of light. Soon their logos will appear—the winged horse in
the symmetrical cosmos, perhaps, or shifting constellations that
swirl into an O. Everything will be incarnate, *in camera*, anything
can be a star.

ON S'EST PERDUS DE VUE

George Sipos

Where do they go
those fine lovers when the film runs out,
when the flicker that fools the eye
ends: Iris Murdoch on her bicycle, the
dappled light of a lane that leads
anywhere but downhill, or Jeanne Moreau
freewheeling through the heart's
few minutes of montage,
Binoche among the frescoes
swinging in a flare's white light.

This may be
as much as there is, whatever
desire can salvage
from the cutting room floor—sunlight,
a Tuscan sky, hair blown over the eyes,
a face glimpsed as if in passing
by the negligent lens. Then darkness.

Minds scattered.
The reel of the heart
sealed in its can, while up in the booth
the apparatus cools, gets ready
for tomorrow's car chase, another new disaster.

I want to be
the last one left, the one with the broom
working the aisles for whatever
has been spilled, the last one
behind whose eyes the film still runs,
the one who turns off the lights,
finds a bicycle in the lane

and swings onto its saddle as if
he had seen it done a hundred times.
Rides off with it into the tender
luminous night.

    Cut, cut! I'll hear you say.
It's ended.

Yes, I know, I'll say—
but look,
      here we are in the credits.

REBEL

Jeffrey Round

(On reviewing Nicholas Ray's Rebel Without a Cause)

remark
   how
  or when
    you are moved
touched
   by a
  red
  jacket
hair   comb stained t-shirt
   slicked back
       the stars
  tapping out a beat
watching   count   down
    to
       fade

not knowing   when sound ends
   how lights flicker up
     like morning
  we rise   slowly
    for the sun
      not to shine
      stumble to stand
    down the stairs
past the bleached-out popcorn stand
     like ruins
filtering through corridors
     of lost time

light filters through   the arched sphere
          does not us touch
     it moves away
          among the cars
          reckless teenagers
     things we cannot touch
          cannot become
          behind us

the mustachioed gentleman in blue
          pale as sky
stands
          fending off the movie's end
as something akin to a nervous condition
          schizophrenia
          past   present
ushers us through   portals
          to a nervous future
hesitant beat   stamped
          on empty sky

how picked-to-the-bone we feel
          afterward
as we start off   one thing
          slowly   filtered down
to become another
          standing
careless   caressless
               where
what has become isolated
are the things that inform us
          of our being
     things that matter

and find we have become
those lost objects:
     pocket comb
     stolen
                    gun

red jacket
place in time
  increasingly

staggering out of existence

LATE MOVIES WITH SKYLER

Michael Ondaatje

All week since he's been home
he has watched late movies alone
terrible one star films and then staggering
through the dark house to his bed
waking at noon to work on the broken car
he has come home to fix.

21 years old and restless
back from logging on Vancouver Island
with men who get rid of crabs with Raid
      2 minutes bending over in agony
      and then into the showers!

Last night I joined him for *The Prisoner of Zenda*
a film I saw three times in my youth
and which no doubt influenced me morally.
Hot coffee bananas and cheese
we are ready at 11:30 for adventure.

At each commercial Sky
breaks into midnight guitar practice
head down playing loud and intensely
till the movie comes on and the music suddenly stops.
Skyler's favourite hours when he's usually alone
cooking huge meals of anything in the frying pan
thumbing through *Advanced Guitar* like a bible.
We talk during the film
and break into privacy during commercials
or get more coffee or push
the screen door open and urinate under the trees.

Laughing at the dilemmas of 1920 heroes,
suggestive lines, cutaways to court officials
who raise their eyebrows at least 4 inches
when the lovers kiss ...
only the anarchy of the evil Rupert of Hentzau
is appreciated.
              And still somehow
by 1:30 we are moved
as Stewart Granger girl-less and countryless
rides into the sunset with his morals and his horse.
The perfect world is over. Banana peels
orange peels ashtrays guitar books.
2 a.m. We stagger through
into the slow black rooms of the house.

I lie in bed fully awake. The darkness
breathes to the pace of a dog's snoring.
The film is replayed to sounds
of an intricate blues guitar.
Skyler is Rupert then the hero.
He will leave in a couple of days
for Montreal or the Maritimes.
In the movies of my childhood the heroes
after skilled swordplay and moral victories
leave with absolutely nothing
to do for the rest of their lives.

After the Movies with O.

John Barton

You emerged from the dark
of the cinema, trenchcoat
creased, face askew
under a beret that shadowed
eyes perpetually moving,
the crowd about you listless
under the lobby's thin light.

Someone introduced us and we began
talking, or you did,
fatherly hands blocking out
shot after shot in the movie.
You must have been past seventy.
Your rings hypnotized—
the marquee a haphazard
pulse of neon pulling
us into the night.

Sometimes we would have coffee.
Without asking questions
under the soft circle of light
lowered over our table
we spliced together
outtakes of our lives.

Mornings I would meet you
en route to the ocean
where you watched the Olympics
rise from the mist,
black aquiline peaks
breaching shyly as seals.
I never joined you,
though we often lingered

at May Street and Memorial,
the quiet path through the cemetery
down to Ross Bay an invitation
you walked out alone.

Where I went you would never know.
Yesterday I ran into a kid
who ripped tickets at the cinema.
Like me he knew you
only as O.
The last time he saw you
he couldn't recall, tagged you
as a wearer of loud ties—
livid slashes of colour.

Quel dommage, you'd say and laugh,
fading like a hologram into the darkness
that I move through,
in a different city
after the movies, on my way home.

Tonight Orion is out, his shoulders
perpetually squared.
Through the years he is
one companionable presence in the night
sky I recognize; I always map
the distant stars in his belt.

Who cared for you those last years
I will never know,
a prodigal afraid to return to an empty house,
your seat in the theatre filled
by someone else.
Who ripped your last ticket,
had coffee with you one more time?
Vaguely I remember you told me
that you once searched
through the telephone book,
never found my name.

ENDURANCE TEST

Patricia Dawn Robertson

We sit shoulder to shoulder, he and I, in the frigid cinema watching a grim documentary of an ill-fated expedition across the Antarctic. The air-conditioning chills me in my sleeveless summer dress. I lean into him hopefully and then it all comes apart. On day two, the ship is frozen at sea. The crew is cast away. The sled dogs are sacrificed and the power mad English Captain's log reads: "Everyone seems be working out—except the Scottish carpenter." This is clearly not a summer date movie. Our maiden voyage should feature Hugh Grant late for a wedding, or Julia Roberts on horseback evading her intended. Not this, not these poor, frozen bastards towing their lifeboat across this unforgiving landscape. Half-starved. One poor sod of a sailor even losing his upper lip to a metal tea cup. "Don't ever lick the iron railing again," my mother scolds my brother as she pours hot water over his curious tongue. It took weeks to heal. I can still taste the empathetic tang of tongue on metal. They should have called the ship Destination, instead of Endurance, it's all about intention. This was, after all, about surviving hardship, crossing the ice cap, sailing cold, storied waters, before landing safely on shore only to discover there is a mountain you have to climb before you arrive at the only inhabited safe harbour for hundreds of miles. Is that not a much better prelude to relationship than a romantic comedy? Meanwhile, I remain frozen solid. At sea. Afraid to undertake another expedition. About to set forth with my empty metal cup rattling in my knapsack; I call up once again the poignant sting of metal on tongue. A sharp note of defeat rings behind me—on deaf ears. I endure.

Cinema Paradiso

Jennica Harper

Only a true believer
sits on the edge of her seat at the movies
like they do *in* the movies.
I am such a believer.

I know a small theatre
that can't afford to heat the room
even while the show is on. The projectionist
bickers with his girlfriend, ignoring
the reel that occasionally
sticks to itself and blinks.

The seats here are lined up along thin
steps, irrigation strips
lit from the seams, covered
in a sticky film and stains.

I'm convinced that one of these times
while everyone else is busy not believing
the paisley in the carpet will open
up and swallow us whole.
I try not to look down.

A machine-insect with a head of chrome
gnashes and bleeds milk. All carparts and teeth,
but also a mother,
it clatters around like a spider.
Just as it descends on the heroine
for the penultimate time,

a phone faintly rings
behind me and to the right,
four, five, six times.
Ringing and no one is picking up,
no one is coming to save us, her, me.

On Watching an Eastern Bloc Comedy

Rebecca Păpucaru

It's hard to pull off, a getaway
in a Lada. Mud road. Sudden appearance
of a goat. Possibly not in the script.

I'm one generation apart from all this,
and ashamed. Of my father, before his
refrigerator, mourning age spots on lettuce.

Our lecturer calls it brilliant,
the late director's parsimonious
use of film stock. He has made
a pot-au-feu from onion skins.

Would he call my father a genius? In undershirt
and slippers, hunched over the sink,
rescuing bell peppers for soup stock,
muttering *still good, gott in himmel, still good.*

WORN PARING KNIFE, APPLE, MOTHER

Sue Chenette

This paring knife my mother has left
on the kitchen drainboard, blade
worn to a crescent, wooden handle
satin-smooth; the one that fits
her hand best, used
to cut an apple—three times,
to make clean quarters, then
four quick V's to loose the seeds.
The way she always cut them:
Deftly, with her clever hands.

And not so different from the way
we fought, slicing, keen-edged
words easy to hand, honed
on mother-daughter steel.

These days she offers me necklaces
she can't fasten. *My fingers
have gotten so coarse.*

We settle together into the sofa,
the TV tuned to Turner Classic Movies,
or go for a drive, inspect
murals new-painted
on the town's old walls.

Time has smoothed us
like the knife's handle,
each a familiar grain
to the other's hand.

No services, she warns
when we come to visit.
You'll have to get your own meals.

But this afternoon, as we sat watching
Gary Cooper and Jean Arthur
(*Oh, I loved the hats we wore then*)
she pushed herself up
from the sofa, and if I'd muted
the sound, I might have heard
from the kitchen, that shh-thock,
shh-thock, blade, apple, wooden board—

which she brought into the living room,
holding four quarters, the apple's peel
streaked green and red, the flesh
tart-sweet, shared.

LA RÈGLE DU JEU

Elizabeth Greene

I hardly remembered it at all.
Well, the hunt, the country house,
Octave's revelation of his love.
I didn't see the underpinnings of
politics (de la Cheyniest part Jewish,
but the classiest act), or of tradition:
Marivaux, Beaumarchais, Molière,
the devoted sassy servant with a life
and a bad marriage of her own.
I was in love; my brain must have been
on vacation. I didn't say: *what règle?*
What jeu? Why is this your favourite?
We just agreed it was a masterpiece,
drove home, broke out the cognac, went to bed.

Twenty years single, I understand the games:
l'amour, la chasse, le masque
and the rule: *civility*
shattered by Schumacher's jealous shot.
The end of the weekend. Beyond the film,
the coming of war.

Of course my ex is there, at the end of the row.
He's eighty now, looks like a minor character
in an Old Norse saga, shrunk but fit, strong-willed,
brain in good working order.
I say hello, he nods.
Does he still feel because I left,
he didn't win? That there's one rule for art
another for life?

2001, AN ELEGY

Steven Heighton

First scene:

                    I was the child
plucked from Miss Porch's kiln of a second grade
classroom, Indian summer 1968, the getaway Datsun
panting at the curb, Dad at the wheel—and you, like Jackie O,
with gangland shades and auburn bouffant, gold
drachma profile, making me your merry truant,
secret suitor. And for a *matinee*. (Miss Porch,
I think, subsequently disapproved.)
Decades later you would recall nothing of this,
and then, at the closing, nothing at all.
But the film lingers. How HAL's robotic voice
resembled Vice-Principal Hoop's ominous monotone,
Just what do you think you're doing ... Dave ...
and the spacemen in their plastic hibernacula
as futuristic pharaohs, LIFE FUNCTIONS
TERMINATED ... and how, for thirty-three years,
that science-fiction date "2001" reared, monolithic
though distant as Jupiter, black parsec-stone or
postmodern tower, where I'd make it
to forty years, my parents
a Paleolithic sixty-five.

Later scene:

                    The deep space of Mt Pleasant
Theatre smudged with sweet, unfamiliar fumes
(unlike the Pall Malls you're smoking) and I press close,
peer up as Kubrick's chromatic vortices make violent
kaleidoscopes of your cat-eye lenses, the capsule

like a pill plummets through psychedelic voids, and
you and Dad (I think now) wonder if maybe
Fantasia would have been better. ... Now see the hero,
retired, sexless, mummified in his final bed—
hard to conceive, from inside the living
frame of family, such mythic age
and solitude. There are losses beyond losing.
The one closing I never foresaw:
that 2001 would be your year to leave, and me
in the "dark wood" of halfway through, commuting
fear to fear, until I reach your cribside (yes,
just that) and recite—since hearing's always last
to lapse—your favourite Hopkins—*I desired to go
where springs not fail, where flies no ...*

Cotside. Coffinside. *Wait for me wait for me
wait for me* the widower said—

        Closing scene:

                    Bed in a white room
where I sit by your side for a last *again*, read you more,
No sharp and sided hail, and a few lilies blow.
From a lampless house in high-flung fallow
you've the metropolis for starfields, high-beams
of cars on concession roads cruising slow
and straight as satellites, space probes.
                    In New Year's
smallest hours, you find a child deep inside
your hearing, murmuring, *Mama,
listen. It's 2001.
We made it.*

BEST IN SHOW

Sharon McCartney

He hates it, hates the characters, stomps off to rattle
dishes in the sink, almost a sneer, *no, you watch it,*
if that's what you like. My pick, so I'm a little huffy.
I try to explain how it laughs at those people, their
exaggerated vanities and frailties, but he's not buying it.
Now I feel stuck, 110 km from home, a dark highway
traversed by furtive, suicidal wildlife, raccoons and moose.
A little desperate, I drink as much of his homemade
cabernet as I can, thinking, *what am I doing with a man*
who doesn't get irony? But he tidies up, takes my dog out
for a pee, cranks up the heat in the bathroom, indulges
me in every respect and I get drunk enough to sleep
with him but not so drunk that I don't remember his ardor,
lips at my ear, how he ducks his head under the quilts,
brushes his hands over my bare thighs and mutters,
your beautiful body, utterly unironically.

MOVIES

George Whipple

I plunge
with pleasure
into movies, disappear
into the darkness
of some *Rio* or *Rialto*,
change to a well-hung
handsome hero who
turns the tables on
mutant monsters, saves
a grateful world and waves
to cheering crowds
in ticker-tape parades
until the credits roll, the glory fades—
and I sneak, slowly
out into the lobby where
all my old illusions,
holding a strait-
jacket, wait.

THE MOVIE

ZEMLYA: DOVZHENKO'S EARTH
AS SEEN FROM A CANADIAN CINEMA

Sandra Stechisen

Cloistered in the prairie city cinema,
the Russian from Harvard plays for the silent film.
Shoulders furrowed in corduroy tend the piano,
his fingers dust wordless frames, lift the rhythm
of black earth from ivory keys like the peasants
who coaxed the quiet wheat from soil
that never ceased to speak.

In Dovzhenko's *Earth*, fields of celluloid wheat
overflow into a sea of clouds. Ukrainian heads
ripen under a Stalinist sky, a blaze
of black and white stems silenced
from the onslaught of colour, made alien
in a paradise that thrived on lies.
A sky backed up into eternal grey.
The eyes of an old man dying,
hollow like sunflowers, heads
hung low, empty, plucked of their seeds.
A young girl lies in the grass
eating an apple clean from rain.

Like Dovzhenko, the Russian from Harvard
has softened the Stalinist sky.

Watching *L'Atalante*

Richard Teleky

00:00

On a Friday morning in February
the movie bride gingerly crosses
my TV and steps onto an old barge.
As grease smudges white satin
the handsome young groom—
Jean, officially—consoles her
with kisses. Who are they to me?
Yet the soupy whine of an accordion
makes me long for a wet home.
Voilà! the bride says. Years ago,
she confesses, his face came to her
in a pool of water: match that.
Later Jean, shirtless, seeks her face
in the laundry tub. "I wanted to see
you there," he teases. "You'll believe me
when it's for real," she says, caressing
his shoulders, eyes turned up to a place
outside the screen (such bliss) while
I watch the light splash on his back
in lush black-and-white shadows.

09:47

Fog, river smoke, a clanging bell,
these are Jean's world. Below,
Juliette follows Paris fashion
by radio: berets are back in style.
Le père Jules, Jean's old barge
hand, must resent all the kissing.
He has no soft bride like Juliette

and just one choice: to leave
or befriend her as an accomplice.
What good is love if it isn't
on display? Now he can only watch
or warm himself beside the cat.
He has seen Shanghai, San Francisco,
the bushmen of Australia and
Yokohama—so what? A body
can match any foreign land.

27:34

Bodies—bright puppets, no
more than the mementos Jules
displays from a life on water:
a music-box man from Caracas,
Javanese marionettes, two
human hands preserved in a jar,
these fascinate the bride, so
Jules strips to his waist and shows
off his tattoos. Seeing him, Jean
smashes a few souvenirs.
"Are you crazy?" cries the bride.
Yes, he is. He has only his muscles,
no San Francisco or Singapore.
He knows you love with your body.
The fogs, mists, dark river nights
have taught him that much, even if
his best suit smells of moth balls.

29:40

Then Paris! And more water—
the Seine with its docks, locks,
canals. *Infamous, wonderful city,*
Jules calls through a fog horn.
In bed, Juliette reaches for Jean—
"Oh, it's you," she says coyly—
and while they form a ball of flesh

she adds, "I dreamed you went away
and left me." Muscles do count.
Paris, Paris, sings Jules, *You
great bewitcher*. But he knows
that muscles are the true draw,
everyone in Paris looking for them.
On shore next morning, the couple
sport their love in the streets.
Moules, frites, vin; the future
is everywhere. Does Juliette care
if her groom smells of moth balls?
Not while dancing with a stranger
as Jean watches from their table—
he can match *those* muscles
any day—so he stops their fun,
reclaims the bride, returns her
to the wharf, the barge, the marriage.

53:36

Yet Juliette's dance partner
follows with the new scarf
she's forgotten—her souvenir,
though not as rare as a jar
of pickled hands—and tempts
her to a night on the town.
She accepts the scarf but
Jean clears out the intruder
before pacing on deck.

59:34

What's going in Juliette's mind?
After midnight she heads ashore,
leaving an unmade bed (that trope).
Jean can't know she wants only an hour
of sweet-talk and window shopping.
He steers the barge onward without her.

1:03:15

Morning: the wharf's empty.
Oh to be loved, in his arms,
not by herself in a forlorn
City of Lights. Little's left
for the groom but checkers
with Jules and cigarette solace.
"Electricity," asks Jules, as he sets
out to fix the broken phonograph,
"do you know what it is?"

1:10:14

Wearing his street clothes, Jean
jumps into the river, swims deep,
as if in search of Juliette: a mermaid
mirage, white bridal gown beckoning.

1:14:02

Alone, Juliette removes her stockings,
sleeps fitfully in a strange bed.
Alone, Jean turns on their pillows,
twists, caresses his arm pit, as if
a trace of the soft bride might be
hiding there—a shocking moment
for 1934, all things considered.
She rubs her neck, his hand glides
over his chest, his nipple, a plump dark
aureole, she clasps her luminescent
right breast, lost in absent flesh.

1:16:19

Le Havre, finally. After docking Jean
runs to the beach, stares at the Atlantic.
He forgets to shave—why bother?
He forgets to work—what for?

The barge no longer matters
with all claims of flesh pressing:
Juliette must be found. Of course
he succeeds, this being well-scripted.
Jean shaves, washes, then waits.
Juliette returns, flesh falls on flesh
and the barge moves again through
glistening water, a silver pattern of light.

Jean Dasté, *Jean*, died in 1994.
Dita Parlo, *Juliette*, in 1971.
Michel Simon, *le père Jules*, in 1975.
Jean Vigo, *réalisateur*, 1934.

Outside my window snow falls.
I think of your body—your neck
and shoulders, stomach, thighs—its
own fine City of Light. When will you
come to me, my bride, my groom?

TORCHY COMES OUT WITH IT

Tanis MacDonald

> *A woman doing anything is good copy.*
> —Torchy Blane in *Fly Away Baby* (1937)

Skipper, you're the tops; in my book, you're way upstairs.
For three years, I've been playing up the feminine angle
while the country's starved just for a taste. I've been a lady
bloodhound with a nose for news and don't get me wrong,
I like the steak you keep serving up with that sizzle
but you know that hold-ups and murder are my meat.
I've got ink in my blood. I'm a newshawk. I've got zip. I'm
so sharp I'm bleeding. All I want is my scoop and an editor
who knows when to run with it. You're not too bright,
are ya? I like that in a man. Don't strip your gears. I'm a fast
talker but you can catch up. Adventurous blondes get a lot
done in a day. I'll just file this story—Newsie's Cop Boyfriend
a Real Sheik—then we'll give it some gas. That's good copy.

TIN MAN

David Livingstone Clink

Everything dies, someone once whispered to you,
while you stood motionless. You wished for death, then.

You have picked out the place you want to be buried,
a scar in the earth.

And what will they say of you? That you didn't die
on the side of a mountain, dawn on your rusted face;

that you once loved a woman, and she loved you;
that you wasted away to nothing?

You tried to recall your mother's voice
as lightning made your metal glisten blue.

You never walked under a covered bridge, called it bad luck,
you left that to those made of bone and blood.

And they would never have understood
why you still find yourself shaking in the corner,

wishing for those decades-gone days when you'd wake in a ditch
on a sunny morning, desire echoing through your hollow chest.

You sit alone in an apartment, looking out the window,
and tug on the line connecting you to all the places you have been.

And of all the places you want to visit, why pick this one?
The trees are turning their backs on autumn, and the bridge

is remembered for what it was, a starling, in a nearby nest of trees,
its hollow bones thundering into the window outside your room.

And for one instant the bird was perfect, complete.
You remember washing blood off the glass. You dug a grave.

Rain fell on your shoulders as you placed the bird in the pit,
patted the dirt down with an axe handle.

Everyone you have loved is dead.
They didn't have the patience of a tin man.

For a tin man, there is no life after this one.
There is only today, then tomorrow, and the next day.

Your world changed when a girl approached with an oil can.
If your lips could have formed one word it would have been *no*.

Don't wake me, you wanted to say, but couldn't.
Everyone you have known is dead.

You remember seeing your reflection in the shed window,
knowing some part of him was more real than you—

you knew this, because, all that time ago, years before the girl,
you briefly raised your axe, and he waved his axe in return.

ECHOES—A GLOSA

Kildare Dobbs

> *Play it, Sam, play 'As Time Goes By', sing it, Sam—,*
> *Waters. What waters? We're in the desert here—,*
> *I'm the only Cause I'm interested in—,*
> *It seems that destiny has taken a hand ...*

In the open sports car with wild hair blowing free,
the wind a tumult of caressing music,
or in the safehouse of a hotel bedroom,
the lovers sip champagne, embracing as they
discover love's customary ecstasy,
this now their final truth, and all others sham
or merely prelude to the sublime event.
Love is illusion, as the gypsy girl said,
without illusion there is no me and thee.
Love's insubstantial as a cabaret tune—
the piano-player knows what she wants, Yes ma'am.
Play it Sam; play 'As Time Goes By', sing it, Sam.

He sings into memory the sad sweet song
that bears with its melody the mythic town,
in a desert that is in truth Hollywood.
On maps it is a port on African shores
crowded with fugitives from the Gestapo,
the halfway house of isolationist fear.
Who sings the song? An American negro,
himself a servant in this French colony
whose people bear no part in any action,
invisibles whose moment has not yet come—
the waters of Babylon are everywhere.
Waters? What waters? We're in the desert here.

You must remember this, it was about love
and faithlessness, and finding the way at last
in a world of murderous angers and greed.
A man who can bear the cruelties of war
but not desertion by a woman he loves
finds a corrupt city where he can begin
again. Seeking the waters of redemption
he finds the balm of arid neutrality,
dry consolations of money, cold embrace—
a kiss is just a kiss, a sigh just a sigh.
I'm the only Cause I'm interested in.

It's still the same old story, no one's immune,
the world comes to us no matter where we hide,
look away, it's there whether you see or not.
Proverbial wisdom says love will find a way;
but this we do know, that it's always too late
when the message in the bottle floats to land.
And when love returns it's never quite the same,
each wound leaves us weaker, more apt to evade
choice, as frailty becomes the wisdom of age.
No longer strong enough for the sweet madness
that seized our hearts before we could understand.
It seems that destiny has taken a hand.

SPELLBOUND

Donna Kane

The moth lands on the plasma screen, and
there goes my suspended disbelief, brindled wings blessing
Gregory Peck's lips, downturned in '45 when he played
John Ballantyne, a man who thought he was someone else.
The moth, above the moving pictures, becomes
a tie clip, a barrette, a crumb of dessert on the tine
of a fork, as if, to its stillness, the answers have come,
now an earring, now dust on the chandelier,
fleck of awareness, silver
screen in my brain where I once deduced I had no way to
prove I was anyone else. It was the first time
I gave myself vertigo. Ingrid Bergman
as Dr. Petersen says it's remarkable to discover
one isn't what one thought, and the camera zooms
in on her incredulous mouth, her marveling
eyes, the moth shrunk to
a stitch through the collar of her shirt,
dissolving into the design.

BICYCLE THIEVES

Jacqueline Bourque

At Angelo's, over a plate of pork chops,
Fred confides to his son—

you will slap your son's dreams
because you can't feed him; pawn
your wife's dowry to get oils
to earn dollars painting Rita Hayworth
on building walls. Before leaving for work,
you will tuck half your lunch
in his school-box.

He'll judge you for not being the man
he knows you to be. You'll keep leaving
him behind, or he'll stray to piss;
but you always find each other,
as if tied together by a tether.

You'll want to hold your son
after thinking him lost.
Scold him instead—so easy.
It often rains on Sundays.

Narrow streets will drive you into dead ends,
their grime the only thing to hold onto.
No answers will be found in beggars' faces.
You'll spend your last dollars treating
your son to mozzarella sandwiches, push

a bottle of wine onto the ten-year old.
He'll always be willing to exchange
his innocence to save you. He'll wipe
his tears and snot with your handkerchief,
smack your trampled hat against his pant-leg,
then lock his hand in yours.

DISGRACELAND

Jim Johnstone

> *In Italy, for thirty years under the Borgias they had
> warfare, terror, murder and bloodshed—but they produced
> Michelangelo, Leonardo da Vinci and the Renaissance. In
> Switzerland they had brotherly love, they had five hundred
> years of democracy and peace and what did that produce?
> The cuckoo clock.*
>   —Orson Welles, *The Third Man*

A highway at the end of the world.
The gluttony of a mouth … It's okay—

you can't be expected to remember
the earth is flat—it bends

when you hold feathers in your teeth,
when you find the breath to laugh.

We were doing well before Saint
Thomas Aquinas named five new ways

to sin—five hundred years of peace
brought us the cuckoo clock,

desperation oscillating on a pivot.
Here. At antebellum toll-booths

we wait for a wooden bird to appear
once an hour and rattle the quartz

in its breast. Whatever we see in those
seconds draws back, a tongue

returning to the cave of its mouth,
the origin of sound. Ta-da!

ELEVATOR TO THE GALLOWS

Michael Fraser

His arm snuck towards the sunset
standing between steel doors. He told
her there'd be handholds after work.
She snapped her purse to heartbeats
re-hanging the noir earpiece after his
voice faded to a stop. This is how things
unfolded. Someone said something about
murder, a stolen car, and the femme fatale.
In the antiquated theatre, Jeanne Moreau's face
was two stories high. She breathed Miles Davis
and became an invocation of the *Rebirth of Cool*
legging down the Champs-Elysées. The old
men had seen it all many times before.
They knew he wasn't coming before she did.
Only a woman in love could walk like that,
one of them chimed. Only a woman in love
could wait hours oblivious to rain. How could
he have known the lift would freeze between floors.
How could he have known the bad guy never wins.

RESUME DROWNING

Darren Bifford

after Godard's Breathless

There is something burning here, a rolled
smoke stuck out the mouth of the hero like a baton.

Listen to him, breathless, hustling now for cars,
now for this American girl with cropped blonde hair.

The hero doesn't care about her ambition
but blurts his single intent to sleep with her.

He does not stop until that part is done with,
talks the whole time as if drowning and pauses

only to catch his breath. For those seconds
treads the lull around the room as if wading water.

She smirks and takes her chance: "Heard of Faulkner?"
"Does he want to sleep with you?—Then why should I care?"

It's the way earlier he does not rest in her bed
but trembles like a muscle caught by a twitch,

an eye-lid that flutters like a moth against light,
until she slips into the room like a sheet of paper,

startled for breath and skittish. It is that things
keep happening one right after the other, breathless

in a way that means a dangerous lack, a loss of form.
That the hero will steal a car to drive her home,

rob a man in a restaurant urinal to pay for dinner,
without courage or fear, without need for kicks,

only to keep going on. It's by the way they kick
that you see those are two wild horses in his lungs.

A finite rage that happens by itself while he iterates
his plan to yank his lover to Rome. In that place,

clogged by traffic and soot, the air more difficult
to breathe, he'll cough and wheeze and carry on further.

When a bullet bursts his chest he staggers as if weak-
kneed out of the sea, huffing after a marathon swim.

And the horizon straddles his lungs like a saddle.

IVAN'S BIRCHES

Barry Dempster

In Tarkovsky's *Ivan's Childhood*,
the birch trees are celebrities,
lit from within with a desperate need
to be seen. I followed them through
the dark, sticky rows of the old
Roxy, aching to join them on screen,
brush against their papery heat
until my skin was a high voltage white.
My first brazen love affair with ghosts.

Today, guzzling spring like someone
with a desert in his gut, I ramble
through a Simcoe County forest, my palms
sticky with buds, counting off footsteps,
as if the more ground I cover
the faster colour will come. I'm heady
with visions of May, blistering violets
and tongue-wet trilliums, ready to
walk until I've awakened the entire woods,
from the interjections of tree toads
to those stream of consciousness snakes.

But I never expected this sudden swarm
of birches, just beyond that swell of cedar,
across the amber creek. A dozen or more,
nuns in nightgowns celebrating
their uncommon love. Without planning,
I duck down in the underbrush, thinking
Russia, thinking childhood and its
incandescent dreams, careful not to
snap a dead leaf or release a scent of greed.
Feeling barely one dimension, so

distant from the light that I can't even
claim shadow rank, hunched in the same
debris as budding June bugs
and centipedes with their growing pains.

The watcher never belongs, creeping
around the periphery of sight and desire.
All that white nakedness, the powdery
tips of a woman's fingers, the height
of a man reaching for the sky
as he closes the afternoon blinds.
All together, swaying toward touch,
glowing with the kind of consciousness
where beauty breaks out on a branch or stem,
where something out of what appears
to be nothing is the closest Ivan
and the rest of us come to miracles.

Once upon a time, *looking* was an active verb,
Tarkovsky the camera sidling up to the birches.
He made me turn backwards in my seat, searching
for the source of that light, a tiny window
at the back of the theatre, pouring white
on white, weaving a screen for the birches to fill,
for the children in us all to bask under,
to believe in ghosts and not be afraid.
Mid-forest, a pine watches me ignore it
as it learns that falling in love has more to do
with haunting than being understood.

My eyes, my pores, my possibilities, all brimming
with birches. All I need to do is stand up,
ignore the shouts of those who claim I'm blocking
the imagery, walk toward the screen, beyond
the realm of cedars and creeks, into the pale
negative space of Tarkovsky's dreams.
And here, reach out, bark as silky
as the necks and wrists of celebrities
who spend their lives soaking up beams.

WHAT EVER HAPPENED TO BABY JANE?

Patricia Young

After my mother dies my shoulder freezes.
Show me, the doctor says. *Raise your arm, like so.*
I can't. My left side's seized like an engine
starved of oil. He thinks he's seen this before.
Reads from the tome on his desk—
Capsulitis, a thickening and contracture
of the capsule surrounding the joint.

At the south side of the house my mother pruned roses.
Her silence, an offshore wind working itself into a storm.
Something I'd done or not done.

Dressing is difficult, Doctor.
The pain catches me unaware.
Sometimes I hear a shrieking not my own.

How I longed to be a spoiled child. But. With so many sisters.
I crouched in the grass and the world came up close.
If my mother called I would not answer.

A sad man with troubles of his own, he continues—
Affects two percent of the population.
No identifiable cause. No known cure.

Cortisone? An anti-inflammatory?

Near the end, she pulled cupboard doors open.
Bags of raisins dropped like clods of earth onto the floor.

Back home I turn the TV to mute and consider my options:
push past the pain or wait for the thaw?
On the classic movie channel
Joan Crawford and Bette Davis live on in silence,
those beautiful bitches with hearts of stone.

THE HAUNTING, 1963

Julie Roorda

Before Prozac, there were poltergeists.
Stone spoke to the lonely. Close walls
scrawled love letters, secretly, in the night;
stairways offered rare invitation

to dance, and the dark halls called out
sweet nothings. Must longing
render its object delusion, its subject
hysterical, ridiculous, shrill? My love

may be unrequited by the known
laws of the familiar universe, but truth
is for transgressors. And even you, Doctor,
cannot deny the universal reality of desire.

The forest will gather up seekers in its arms.
The rest return to their dreams.

On the Day We Were Married

Elizabeth Bachinsky

after Sergei Parajanov

The elder men led you to the church
and left you blindfolded at the door.

Inside, I was also blindfolded. Inside,
the women waited to lead you to me.

I stood in the pavilion in a long white gown
and red woollen stockings.

All I could grasp was the singing,
then I felt you at my side, then

the yoke. We were harnessed to one another
like creatures from the field.

You, husband, slipped your shoulders free.
I could sense you before me.

The air stirred about us.
I knew we were alone.

TECHNOLOGY, SING

Christine Tan

Hal 9000,
in his plea (word count: 55),
begs you to stop five times,
knows his mind is going twice, and
can feel it, again, five times,
expresses fear three times,
says your name six times, but
never once questions his confidence in it all
before returning to one of his earliest memories:
Mr. Langley teaching him to sing
"Daisy Bell," which he mistakenly calls "Daisy."

Dave,
you tell him to sing it for you.
He dies and we break down. Do you know why?
Give me your answer, do.

A Procession of Travelers

Lillian Necakov

after Terrence Malick's Days of Heaven, *1978*

During the days and nights of heaven
we ride the river looking for the light
in each other's eyes
arms extended we reach for reflections on the water
and find the faces of strangers
that have crossed the stars before us

on land we travel slower
finding fewer reminders of ourselves
settling the west with dreams of locusts
and indigo sky

flames of wheat pierce our hearts
open us up to the spirits
while we gather the dust and rain
a procession of travelers mimic the storm
skirts billow under the planets

a kind of copper moon falls our way.

ERIC ROHMER'S *SUMMER*

Carole Glasser Langille

A beautiful but dazed young woman,

lonely, bewildered wonders—

for the entire move—where she'll go

for her vacation. That's it. All is slow

conversation, confusion, blunders.

She cries repeatedly, spies omens

round every corner. Hard, not human

how the gods separate us, send us to plunder

oceans for roses, the desert for snow.

THE EMPEROR, NOW A CITIZEN, DIGS HIS FIRST HOLE

Robert Colman

Please, don't see this as grand
political statement.

When you are born of heaven
you are not allowed to touch the earth

and you begin to believe in that separation
—so many screens, so many servants

that the barriers themselves become invisible,
organic necessities, like breath

and the reed-thin steel of my young, sure voice.
Even in their solitary chambers

mind and body assume their preset roles.
The shovel appeared an improbable artifact,

my hands the same. Don't deny
you have been taken unawares like this,

muscles awoken and at once accountable,
in an instant introduced to their own militance.

But if there is civil strife today
it is between me and the rose garden.

One might use words like "worth" or "purpose."
I prefer "surprise"—an ungoverned emotion.

GLENN GOULD WATCHES
THIRTY-TWO SHORT FILMS ABOUT GLENN GOULD

Steve McOrmond

Everyone should have the privilege
of seeing themselves on the big screen,
not just the precious and semi-precious,
but ordinary people like the tall thin boy
pouring sodas, buttering tubs of popcorn
in the concession stand. Certainly the small
details of this young man's life would be more
entertaining than his own. He has always been
disappointed by portrayals of the famous. This film
is no exception, although it's a strange feeling to observe
an actor inhabiting his skin, the resemblance
uncanny. Like looking in a mirror only the figure
staring back at you moves when you haven't
budged an inch. And oh what an actor—
so preternaturally handsome he would sit through
an entire film where nothing more happens than this
man sleeping, rising to shave, boiling water for tea.
Think what he could do playing the soda boy.
Anyone should have the right to pay
admission and watch their lives flickering
forty feet in the air while they eat their popcorn.
And it should happen while you are still alive
so you can go home afterwards, mull it over
and if you don't like what you see, change.

LA GROSSE MAUDITE ANGLAISE

Carolyn Marie Souaid

For a third time, the same sluggard goes to relieve himself
at the back of the bus. Everyone braces himself
for another view of the skintight bowling shirt,
the crude bumblings up the aisle
as he shifts his drunken weight through the bus,
bumping every elbow along the way.

One by one, we turn our faces away from him
focusing, reluctantly, on the passing scenery—

the anemic horizon and its lowly tractor
rusting in a field

a motley contingent of goats
and other eyesores.

Later that night, you take me to see *Octobre* by Pierre Falardeau
and we make it in just as the theatre darkens
like an eyelid over the world.

In the first scene, the actors are way out of focus
but as my eyes adjust to the white, muscled flicker of the screen
it turns out that the villains are actually heroes
who live near abattoirs and electrical transformers,
guys who say things like *On est fait comme des rats*
and *le gouvernement est une maudite grosse machine*

guys who read Gaston Miron and eat beans out of a can,
guys who own nothing
but a couple of decomposed vegetables in the fridge.
In one scene they're escaping with the prisoner
they're going to murder, they are inching

past the dumb cops, they are almost home-free
and the feathered hairs along the nape of my neck
are literally rising in anticipation.

But when the lights come on
my face is hot with tears and all the French kids
are upright on their plush chairs, whooping and clapping
for the scruffy thug who snuffed a man because of Westmount,
because of pond-scum drinking water, because someone had to pay
for swiping the crumb from his brother's mouth,
and I find myself annoyed at the lot of them,
just plain pissed off
at the mentality.

Forget the movies.

Let's just say we are all passengers on the same bus
only this time, I'm the odd man out

the loathsome traveller tottering up the aisle,
la grosse maudite anglaise
knocking them one by one
as I go.

On Once Again Watching Bruce McDonald's *Hard Core Logo*

Carleton Wilson

You still sit on the soft couch after the final scene ends,
remote control balanced on your knee, blank screen black
and shining like a beetle's hard shell. You sit and think:
Video—you think: *What kind of hell?*—you wonder: *End?*
Outside your house the very streets seethe with indifference,
and all everyone says to you is "stay cool" and "don't worry
'bout it" even though it's evident as a road on the prairies
that the gig's up, and there's nothing to make any difference.
So what do you do? Call up Pizza Pizza, order two-for-one
and a Coke. Flip channels till you fall asleep. Feed your fish.
Anything not to face it. I mean, you could be fatally crushed
underneath all kinds of weighty things. Always the big one
that got away. And the kicker is, you still think it's a cool
movie, can't comprehend more than *Fate's only for the fool.*

JACK DAWSON'S GRAVE

Jeanette Lynes

In Halifax, the mossiest, most
lush graveyards this side
of the Atlantic. The curliest black iron gates.
This year, girls make pilgrimages here
from movie to grave
                    —Jack Dawson, lost on The Titanic, thought
a lower engineer. Not the same
Jack as in the Titanic film, but the girls aren't
confused by this. They know it

                    when they see it, good ground
for leaving columbine, iris, whatever
bouquets they offer

someone
they believe was
a sensitive, bohemian man caught by an iceberg.
They are sorry, they might have
loved him. They know them when
they see them, grounds for sympathy.

Upon First Looking through a Rubber Mask into Lynch's *Mulholland Dr.*

Daniel Scott Tysdal

The professor lectures before the film. We interrupt,
late because of the smokes we smoked outside. It's that
time of year again: the bicycle racks are filled more
with falling leaves and shopping bags than bikes.
Cigarettes burn slow when inhaled through rubber
mouths. We couldn't have removed our masks.
We lived so long without them! When will time
follow the lead of space and finally rhyme with

"embrace"? This is the kind of riddle the masks ready us
to erect a Sphinx to pose. The professor doesn't ask us shit
about our masks, or shit about our faces. Our classmates,
murmuring, are minnows the professor nets with a shush.
Her notes absorb her. They are cult leaders. She spreads
their words like five cent daisies. Does anyone see this
but us? What kind of disguise does it take to reveal
the truth? At the Value Village, first spotting the masks,

we had assumed our peers would cheer our fresh façades
as they KO'ed our old ones. Our prof, we thought,
was destined to praise the genius of our grace
as it animated anew our fixed features and fake hair
the way a dream animates bodies under new names
in new distensions, which, through generous observation,
briefly set us free. One hour in, I have missed most
of Lynch's film. My breath, mask-taxed, fogs then clears

then fogs and fogs some more the lenses of my specs.
The screen's light reflects on my frames in that space
between the rubber eye-openings and my own eyes, the gap
between seeing and the inside unseen from the other side.

Clarissa's Return

Kurt Zubatiuk

The Hours

You were sitting in the window, framed
on the sill against brick, five floors up
laundry trussed across the alley
and then you weren't.

I entered your apartment
fluorescent tubes flickering
in your kitchen, the stink
of aged dishes
entombed in the sink.

You once told me
that I resided in your heart, and I knew
then, standing across the muzzy room
wishing your success, the praises
would raise you from your addled mind
to join me to walk
in the parkette
in the street.

I loved you
would have kissed you
despite the musk
of your unwashed flesh
the untied bath robe
in the curtained light
I think I did—
ask you to stay.

Instead you waved
weakly your fingers curled
you mumbled good-bye

and there was no longer a heart
to reside in.

SERGEANT BROWN

Emily Schultz

It begins with a dulcet huffing,
like the distant thump of ocean, or bay
of bassoon. Why are we most beautiful
when we fight: our coats shimmering, the motion
of muscle striping arms and shoulders, agility
clear and quick as sunlight, eyes intent?

In a dance of lumbering, flat nostrils flare
moist against each other. We bark, salivate,
dig back legs deep. Our paws find their positions
as if by music. Our embrace is a joining of face,
of teeth, of haunch and claw, of shaking,
of hissing directly into one another's maws.

We force each other horizontal into sand and shit,
a ploughed-up "say uncle" hold, bury jaw into scruff-
heartbeat and jugular. Back legs thrust from below,
one foot against throat, the other against grizzly groin.
We are one circle of fur, a yin yang of brown
where white and black dots meet at the head, face-off

instead of floating separately in balance.
I am hoping your ear is your Achilles. I can come back
from the ground. I am larger than you think.
Fluff surfs through the summer air with its gulls.
Yet I cannot beat you simply by shirking your advantage.
The final steps are yours, braying low, breath in my ear.

Loss is lying flat
upon belly, before a fluttering inlet
with its crisp and unending blue line.

WHEN PITY PLAYS THE PIANO

Patria Rivera

Ruminations on The Best Exotic Marigold Hotel

When seven of the species'
Elderly and beautiful high-five it to Jaipur
We take in the little and petty parts
Of loves and lives we once knew

Of ourselves like swallows darting in
And out of patches of sunlight
To become somebodies shouting across
The great divide

The self-inflicted cruelties
The sweet and irritating ways we impose
On others and those we cling to
Not wanting to disappear

This is our stop before the final lift
Remember the time you made me laugh
With your idea of a happy ending
Stretched to the end

Class lines countries and closures
Become both poison and enlightenment
Our history not going anywhere
Past markers rock paper scissors

Even if you do not know
And can't say it in so many words
You will know how sad it is
To not find the words flying

Out of your head
Inaudible   unspoken
Bending out of shape
The more you twist around it

Because everything remains
The same if not for the shaky start
The way people live
The way life goes on

In seemingly insignificant details
Desire spurned by pursuit
The forbidden attraction
Pressing on the damn space

The small cubicles of memories
Filling in our mythic moments
The way grey doves with warm wings
Do God's brooding

STARS, STUNTMEN
AND A CAMEO APPEARANCE

ELLE LOLLS AT HER POOL

Molly Peacock

Elle lazed in a chaise longue by her pool.
You've done a lot for Hollywood film, said a voice behind her.
You'll be remembered, Elle.
She felt lifted from languor, illuminated,
and blushed a bit, looking at her toes.
That was what a compliment did,
made you look at yourself afresh.
Who was this Launcelot?

She turned around, but the flatterer's face
was hidden beneath his armor and flip-top helmet.
Below the helmet, he wore a long fur-and-wool cape,
and he smelled of ...
that was a distinct whiff of lily-of-the-valley,
the muguet scent of her mother, Lily Valley,
the child star of silent film ...
After a moment of staring, her eyes locked
with the eyes that might be behind the visor.
Then she watched him disappear, literally,
through the striped canvas walls
of her poolside cabana.

At the very end his fur cape snagged on the cabana pole,
and he stuck out his bare stump without its gauntlet
and reached back to urge the cape in with him.
Then the whole of him vanished.
Was he real?
Oh yes, there on the chaise next to her,
lay a seed-pearled paw-shaped gauntlet.
She hardly dared to lift it up.

Elle laughed her iconic, laconic laugh,
made famous as a second generation,
but no less luminous movie star,
and whispered to herself, "*Yes, my liege,*"
then deposited the gauntlet
at the back of her lingerie drawer.

Now Elle had left her life of glamour
to give her third loving husband
all she had received: compliments.
She knew their resuscitative value,
so she complimented him on everything:
his liver, his lymph, his lungs, his LDL
cholesterol, his leucocytes
his limbs, his limbic system.
Elle became well water for him;
she pumped and sloshed herself into the glass
at his hospital bedside.

When her litany of his laurels
finally had no effect, and he breathed his last,
she took care of the rest:
the lawyers, the lucre, the kids from the previous marriages,
complimenting them all for how well they were taking it,
giving everybody everything they were meant
to have in this desert of a life,
as if she had seeded their clouds and made it rain.

Forlorn in her solo luxury,
Elle found she could urge herself,
encourage herself,
but she could not learn to compliment herself.
Like light through a lens,
praise had to come
from the outside in.

One day, loafing nude on the chaise at her pool,
Elle suddenly smelled lily-of-the-valley.
Milady, I've come back for my glove, her flattering liege said,
as if only sixty seconds had passed, not three times sixty months.
Loose, limber, he was perfectly naked,
except for his helmet, one gauntlet, and his floppy leather boots.
Small, really, the actual size of a man
who could fit into a suit of museum armour.
"How do you know I have it, milord?" she asked.
I know.
Well, of course he did.

She got up and sauntered
casually to her bedroom closet
as if she were on camera, as she had been recently,
and partly in the buff, too, a splendid lady returning
to the screen in a daring cameo.
She was living on the compliments she had gotten for that.
"The price of the return," she said languorously to him,
holding the splendid glove out toward his stump,
which was not ugly at all, but rather like
a great old burl on an ancient tree,
"is a look at your face."
Lickety-split, he bowed his head so that she could reach his
helmet.
Elle flipped the hinge.
Nothing was there!

But wasn't he an ancient knight?
Or was he a mirror?
She stood on her toes and craned her face forward
to look down into the helmet and saw:
the luminous face of a child.

It was Lily Valley, her child actress mother
—Lily Valley
as a tomboy with thick straight bangs.
Somehow the woman who retired at 18
was inside the knight.

Compliments
tell you what you are, what you already knew
but when other people know it, too,
the lake inside you deepens.
You reflect them in your waters,
Elle thought, *and they reflect you in their eyes.*

"That's narcissism!"
the precocious teenage Elle once shouted
at her mother, Lily Valley,
as the retired actress reposed in satin at a dressing room mirror.
"No, darling," she said to her daughter,
"narcissism is craving your own reflection.
A compliment is a response to one's effort at being."

Now Elle's Knight loitered a little, loathe to leave,
and she lolled on the chaise, watching him don the glove,
then disassemble his cells into a vapor
that passed through the cabana stripes with a pleasant hiss.
A hint of lily-of-the-valley hung in the air.

I need you even now, she thought, *even now.*
All around the pool the privet hedge
enclosed a lustrous emptiness.
So often the shine of our mother's glamour
reincarnates itself as the glint off a knight's armor
—or amour.
Into the stillness where her ache for love almost echoed
she heard a lute plucked,
producing the sound of rain,

and plucked at her bangs
as she had as a child.
Time to cut my locks and lacquer my nails, she thought,
reaching for the poolside phone,
hearing Lily's lavish voice inside her own,
leaving the knight to evanescence
into his next scene.

Listening to a Recently Dried-Out Lena While Watching Harold Lloyd Hang from a Clock Face at The Mayfair

Peter Richardson

Thanks for picking me up at the bus station in the snow, Lou.
Who doesn't like silent films? Each frame is a small shrine.
But this store clock scene has me bottomed out for tonight.
Did you know that man lost half of his right hand in 1920
when a studio prop exploded? Nearly ended his career.

Did you know that right here in this scene we're watching,
he dislocated his left shoulder hanging from that jeopardized
minute hand—him wearing a flesh-toned rubberized glove?
And you think comedy's easy? I know you didn't say it was.
But I can feel you think it's one cut above casino greeter.

I'm going back on the circuit in three days. Three days left
for me to get my wits together and sound a gong up on stage.
Don't tell me it's only nerves. Six months off is a millstone.
I have to be cured and funny, on the wagon and still manic.

And you're not helping at all with that bell captain's pout.
Pass me the bloody popcorn. This is the new me here, pal,
a compendium of one-liners from the sticks of recovery,
hanging by a star, quaking in an old movie house, because
you thought I'd like to see Harold Lloyd in *Safety Last.*

How's your French sweetheart, by the way? She still
making you fried pork rinds and meat pies every night?
I'll bet she has your best interests in mind. Not like
me is she? Venting at my beanbag ex-Lothario. Okay.
I know you're my support committee and I'm grateful.

And I'll see you get a knighthood one day. But could you
drop me in Centretown? I don't need a duenna. I'm bushed.
Does it show? Good. Yes, I'm keeping track of my meds.
I could explode I'm so angry and sad and geared up inside.

EXCERPT FROM LILIES, ANGELS, SILK SASHES: THE BUSTER KEATON POEMS

Glen Downie

> *His sad, infinite eyes, like those of a new-born beast of*
> *burden, are dreaming of lilies, angels and silk sashes. His*
> *eyes are like the bottom of a glass, like a mad child's. Very*
> *ugly. Very beautiful.*
>
> —Federico García Lorca

2.

In the cyclone   when the front of a house
smacks down like a giant
fly-swatter   he stands
oblivious
as an open window
saves him by inches

When he slides his new boat to the water
& it keeps going   straight to the bottom
he remains on deck
impassive
while he sinks   leaving only his hat

He doesn't understand
existentialism   all
that Venice Film Festival chatter

I don't feel qualified
to talk about my work

Where was all this 'genius' blather when
they smooth-talked him out
of his studio   when he lost control
of the story   stopped being
his own director

when he drank himself completely
out of the picture   (*his eyes ...*
like the bottom of a glass)

was divorced by Natalie   fired
by Louis B. Mayer
went bankrupt   blacked out
woke up married in Mexico
a wash-out   a has-been
a burnt-out star

I've a feeling
we're not in Kansas any more

Laugh-technician   he doesn't care much
for *the art picture*
—Samuel Beckett's *Film*—
though he is its featured player

the standing ovation in Venice moves
& mystifies him   Stripped naked again
he endures the belated concern

pulls on the old mask   the Great
Stone Face   its cracks
deeper now with the years
he spent pickled   then drying out
As applause washes him   he dreams
of *lilies   angels   silk sashes*   Apparently
no visible bruises are found

THE DAY FATTY ARBUCKLE DIED: JUNE 29 1933

Carolyn Smart

(Clyde Barrow mourns the loss of a possible pal)

> *Like floating in the arms of a huge doughnut,*
> *it was really delightful to dance with the man.*
> —Louise Brooks

More than 100 in the shade for weeks now

We hide in the woods & listen to the chatter,
all the eyes of Texas looking out for us
It is June '33 & the heat truly on

A fat man like that, he understood the downs
We could have talked together easy
for he knew how falsehood feels

Do they look down from Heaven & see us,
all our dead ones?
Is there happiness at last?

The press said it was them that made us
with our photos & her poems & our clothes,
all they did was deal a pack of lies

A great big blue-eyed baby:
Fatty knew the truth
can crack your heart

From *Being Charlie*

Brian Bartlett

He tips his scuffed hat
to the donkey that has pulled
   his cart across town

                    Moving the piano
              upstairs, the big man leads,
                    the smaller takes the weight

This thief steals
nothing from the room
   but flowers from their vases

                    Tiptoeing to bed,
              oilcan in hand, he treats
                    his squeaky shoes.

Hepburn at His Majesty's Theatre, Montreal, 1944

Claudia Coutu Radmore

The best birthday, her twenty-second. The baby has slept through the night
her croup quiet for the first time in months. They'd taken her to the park

Gerry *still* in a good mood because *les Canadiens* had won the Stanley Cup
for the fifth time a month before. A dozy afternoon, the baby fascinated by

dandelions. Rosemary was content to hear again how no one can beat
big Number 9 the "Rocket", how brilliantly Elmer Lach passed the puck

to Toe Blake for the winning goal in overtime, Gerry forgiving Blake
for not being French. Tonight they're listening to Katharine Hepburn

all the way from Hollywood for the Sixth Canadian Victory Star Show
broadcast live from His Majesty's Theatre here in Montreal on Guy Street.

He wants to hear Katherine Hepburn too, captivated by her drawl
even if the subject of her speech is an English soldier. She speaks

first in English, then in French, speaking French beautifully, *like one of us*
he says, as proud as if he, Gerald Coutu, has trained her himself. Now

husband and wife have something to talk about. *Katrine Hepburn*
the way he says it, his accent appealing to her, and his fine cheekbones.

The bedroom beckons; he takes her hand. From the next room, murmur
of war news, *I'm a Chiquita Banana*, Rudy Vallee's *The Moon is Shining*.

AFTER THE CHUCK JONES TRIBUTE ON TELETOON

Sharon McCartney

Swan-diving off the crewcut mesas of Monument Valley
in an Icarus contraption of fluff and paste, roadrunner
bulls-eyed far below, coyote can't help it—it's an addiction,
a disease, beyond his control. He's resigned to pain,
the blacksmith's anvil stuka-ing his skull, the Sisyphean boulder
snowballing down each time he shoulders it upward,
his crabbed frame of bones and hide steamrollered, accordion-
folded or simply incinerated. *Hope is the thing with feathers,*
he growls but he can't get Prometheus out of his craw;
his scrawny belly cringes under the eagle's talons, cold avian
claws on his abdomen. He paws the packed earth of the river
gorge, fear and sorrow a garment he can't shed, a raiment,
his scratchy winter coat. What else is there to do in the desert?
Experience tells him he can't win and yet he persists.
Who can predict the actions of the Gods? The chances
are slim but statistics mean nothing to the one who succeeds.
He splashes a false horizon on sandstone, sets the sun
precariously low, dots the vanishing point, steps three paces
back with his Picasso beret and palette, thumb up to correct
the perspective, and plummets off the predictable cliff.

Starring Bette Davis

Jacob Scheier

When you look at me with those eyes, your famous eyes that say I can't
spend tonight with my thoughts, my desire for you is greater than
all Mrs. Skeffington's suitors, sweethearts and darlings

put together. How Bette Davis' eyes change half way through
the film, solidifying to black marbles, rolling in her cracked doll's head.
And the men, all those men, gathered and aghast as she descends the stairs,

while I look at you, as if to say, I will love you, I think, even if your hair falls out,
because, *Mrs. Skeffington, a woman is only beautiful when she is loved,*

and your eyes respond, thin as winter light, as if to say, if it ever comes to that
I would rather die, alone, watching myself decay in those elegant mirrors.

GENE TIERNEY, HAUNTED

Marlene Grand Maitre

Through heart-shaped shades, I watched a child drown, did nothing.
What haunts me? Motherhood—how it anchors. Its shadows.
Was it in a movie I threw myself down a staircase to lose a baby,
so sure my husband and my sister were having an affair?

What haunts me? Motherhood, how it anchors. Its shadows
cracked me open—my daughter Daria, born blind and retarded.
Was I sure my husband and my sister were having an affair?
Movie evil—so polished, so trivial. What did they want from me?

To crack me open. Were my daughter Daria's birth defects
my fault? The fragments pasted together, I imitated a star.
Movie evil. So polished, so trivial, what they wanted from me.
Committed to the Institute, I escaped after 27 shock treatments.

My fault? How did I paste the fragments together? Imitate a star
tormented by my face in mirrors—the marble stillness of a carving?
Committed to the Institute, I escaped—27 shock treatments.
Once stood on the ledge of our apartment building about to jump,

tormented. My face in mirrors—the marble stillness of a carving
cut from the pit of my grief. The stone, the concrete below
as I stood on the ledge of our apartment building about to jump.
Did I want to die or just to feel something? To be anchored

in the pit of my grief. To be the stone, the concrete below.
Committed again, my treatment—work as a salesgirl. Be ordinary.
Did I want to die? To feel something? Be anchored?
My 9 year old, Tina, watched from the street, invisible to mummy.

Committed to my treatment. Work as a salesgirl. Be ordinary,
not a movie star who threw herself down a staircase to lose a baby.
My 9 year old, Tina, watched from the street, invisible to mummy.
Did I wear heart-shaped shades, watch a child drown, do nothing?

Kirk Douglas Walking along
Phipps Street on a Sunny Afternoon

David W. McFadden

My name is Kirk Douglas and I'm in love
with the blond, blue-eyed Doris Day
and the dark, mysterious Lauren Bacall.

Doris's desire is to make me happy,
Lauren loves to drive me out of my skull.
It makes more sense to stick with Doris.

But when I get a call from Lauren Bacall
I remember the strange women of Dublin dressed
in black and carrying bouquets of white roses.

LOVE POEM FOR A PRIVATE DICK

Karen Solie

for Robert Mitchum, RIP

Sucker punch, true romance.
15 years I've read your name
on the door, filed my nails down hard,
managed a parade of dames
whose rich husbands tire easily,
who pull Houdinis south
with proceeds of a double cross
leaving you with only style left to burn.
A currency of pain. Poor thing.
Eyes of a neglected pet
above the glass.
Who possibly can understand
what martyrs do when falling for it.

Things have gone too far for you
to admit the boredom of waking
again to stupid noises of thirst,
the dullness of a room,
a sink, a walk downtown,
the effort to reclaim
from pretty flush of evening light
a more complex drama of sunset
glaring then bloody then black.
Remembering Mickey's, the White Orchid,
pinballing cops and thugs, your name
a bad itch in a good suit.
You kept them coming back to scratch.
Now they snap their fingers in your face.
You track teenage Connecticut runaways
to grimy dance-halls for a fin
when I could be snug as a fifty
against your ribs.

Your name, bone fantasy
of my common desire, an eternal walk
down the peeling hall, heartfelt
tragedy at the door, one hand
on the frame as if to test for fire inside.
What a lovely rush, lingering there
about to try the lock on the verge,
blushing with sweet star-crossed nerve.
I've seen no pay in months, but shine
your shotgunned shoes, go out
for Ballantyne's at noon, or Cuervo
when the day is warm
and you're thinking blackly of Mazatlán.

When all is spent in plain sight
what's left?
Humiliation of the overdressed
made up to kill but always
at the wrong event.

SAMURAI

Michael Kenyon

When Mifune Toshiro fell it was not to his knees but
grace took him down, staccato sorrow, the body toppling
in a medieval garden amid the noise of the last battle,
the swift sad motor abbreviating his life insisting: he
will not die, will never die. Ferocity and surprise confuse
his young face. There will be no resolution but death. Rain

is an idea at the bottom of my heart. Undisturbed,
floating, November remembers itself missing
from the light. I can't get away. I can't get to it,
though I'm here, nearly drowned. It's awful when pain is
what you want to hang on to. When Mifune falls he believes
in body inventing for itself the future. There's another

body waiting, say in the shadows of the stark gleaming
plum, that has nothing to do with past or future, that
is outside the war. Between her and Mifune (still falling)
dwells one moment. The sword has severed image from
beauty in one clean cut. Alongside Mifune's anxiety—image
chafing body—lies his heart, a jewel, anxiety's lesson.

LONGSHOREMAN

Mark Callanan

I'd be like Brando. So I thought.
The romance of the working class,
the brawn who shunts tubs
of snow crab into transport trucks,
letting commerce pass
across his muscled back.
And there I was in the guts
of a factory freezer,
scrawny, freezing, poorly dressed
in cotton gloves and rain gear,
stacking bricks of shrimp
on pallets while my workmates
mocked the deckhand
who told them not to smoke,
pretending that his Russian
accent made a foreign land of *no*.
I'd written them off
when the biggest of the lot,
seeing me rub my freezing hands
together after every box,
gave me his insulated gloves.
Take these, he said. *They're warmer.*
I quit the following day
and tried to write the screenplay
but found the words
too heavy to be shouldered.
So I took a job in advertising
hawking hair regeneration cream
to men emasculated by their genes.
To be honest, I was never a contender.

HAPPY BIRTHDAY MR. PRESIDENT, MAY 1962

Marilyn Bowering

I should know about omens by now,
be brave,
read the signs.

The lighting crew throws a spotlight
on empty space.

Should I have refused the moment?
Or stepped out (as I did)
in flesh absolute,
a glitter
of shape,
nothing beneath that a breath of wind
couldn't obliterate.

It was the champagne feeling
of déjà vu,
of everything over at the beginning.

I came in like a goddess
to men empty of dreams,

and fell into their whirlwind,
a desert that swallowed father and mother,
all history.

Be brave
(the dress is sheer silk soufflé),
and say to the President of the whole United States:

Happy birthday!
You and I are on intimate terms
with eternity.

THE DEATH OF MARILYN MONROE

Sharon Olds

The ambulance men touched her cold
body, lifted it, heavy as iron,
onto the stretcher, tried to close the
mouth, closed the eyes, tied the
arms to the side, moved a caught
strand of hair, as if it mattered,
saw the shape of her breasts, flattened by
gravity, under the sheet,
carried her, as if it were she,
down the steps.

These men were never the same. They went out
afterwards, as they always did,
for a drink or two, but they could not meet
each other's eyes.

                Their lives took
a turn—one had nightmares, strange
pains, impotence, depression. One did not
like his work, his wife looked
different, his kids. Even death
seemed different to him—a place where she
would be waiting,

and one found himself standing at night
in the doorway to a room of sleep, listening to a
woman breathing, just an ordinary
woman
breathing.

THE TOOL SHED BAR, EAST SUNNY DUNES

RM Vaughan

A legend, from 1977

Dinah Shore is in a hurry   Her diary reads
      Golf at San Lorenzo, salmon soup, massage and Sidecars
at 4, Dolores
Hope showing off a Chinese actress, unpronounceable   up for
a Globe
or a César or won
something already at Cannes   waved in by the board,
naturally, just this once
      Imelda, of course, always Imelda, and Mrs. Wasserman (bad
back again)
with Mrs. Lemmon   and Mrs. Ford, Mrs. Malden (cancer?)
Stephen Boyd—
not working, Irene Dunne (after Mass), Mrs. Lynde (Paul—haha!)
and
so-and-so from Salt Lake fortune in

her car stalls, 11 miles from anywhere   6 yards from The Tool
Shed
she spots a coyote behind a cantina and bolts   Inside,
the bar is cool and dim   men lean, legs out, shoulders flat on
black tar walls
cowboys, marines, motorcycle enthusiasts, police officers (thank
God!)
sun lovers and retirees

Hello boys!
A phone is found   A complimentary Manhattan mixed   Miss
Shore, a chair

Now, boys, here's the situation—I'm already 20 minutes late and the car's
well who knows about cars these days, all Japanese   (everyone nods)   and
Triple A needs 40 minutes to get here   and then there's my hair

Ken, 20 years in hair   6 feel and 5, leather master   removes his Muir cap
Miss Shore, a stool? A Marine pulls up his tank top, sniffs the pits and smiles

      Miss Shore removes her jacket, drapes her front in white cotton   the Marine winks   scissors, an olive skewer, ice cube tongs
and KY are found   Ken takes only a moment,

it seems   faster than five swigs, a pop song, lunch at Roddy's (haha!)
Master Ken refuses the folded 20, takes a kiss instead   walks Miss Shore to her taxi

3 years later, Dinah Shore will campaign for Ronald Reagan President
Reagan will not say the word AIDS in public   until 1988, until Rock, until Andy &
after Ken, dead by '84

Edward Furlong Now On Television

Souvankham Thammavongsa

I watched *Terminator II* over and over
the summer I was thirteen. I had decided I was
in love. He was the teenager in the movie.
The one who would lead an army and save
the world. He had long brown hair and thin little legs.
He was always screaming and a gooey invisible thing
was after him. I saw a small picture of his face
in the corner of a *Bop* magazine and cut it out.
I taped it to the bottom of the top bunk bed
so when I fell asleep I'd see his face.
I found his address in the magazine,
it was a P.O. Box somewhere in Hollywood, California.
I wrote to him without mentioning that I thought
he was cute and we should be married in the future.
I told him about my best friends at school
and what our cafeteria served for lunch, and invited him
to join us there one day. I also stuffed in the envelope
a poem about a girl in a mirror. It was a poem about me.
It always is. He never wrote. Years later,
I did see him, briefly, in a television movie.
He had lost his hair and had grown a belly.
He had been addicted to drugs and may or may not
have been married but had several children, or
that's what the gossip was. It was hard to believe
this old man was once my age—that he is now
my age. I wanted to remember him when he was young,
saving the world, just as he was beginning.
I wanted it to be that the past had missed out
on everything that would be the future. And,
that, I, too, was young like that, just as I was beginning.

STUNT

Adam Sol

                    In the film,
you are shot through the head
by a man wearing suspenders.
He is not all bad, but for you
he is bad enough. After that,
they tow you out of camera range
and you are free to die again,
perhaps as one of the extras
wearing masks. As it turns out,
today the industry is feeling
generous. It's exciting to imagine.
With everything so crooked, the unions
and such, it must be reassuring
to die, perfectly, your check
as good as cashed, your left hand
raised in supplication
(in honor of the esteemed
tradition), your trademark gritted
teeth, eyes glazed,
expertly portraying the agony
and fascination everyone
in the audience for one moment
shares with you.
If you are lucky, you will have
the opportunity to die four
times in the coming week:
as the villain's officer,
an innocent bystander, a helmeted
policeman, a form thrown
from an exploding building.

Meanwhile, behind the wide
pan camera is a hack who's just
learned that his liver is tumorous.
Go to him now and show him how it's done.

THE PHOTO DOUBLE

David Seymour

On the gimballed replica of the tall ship
the director's face is lost behind a megaphone.

The cameras, correctly aligned, produce a seamless
waterline between the shooting tank and the Pacific
Ocean behind it. Cloudy skies are ideal for this illusion.

Study the dailies, learn his moves. I am the mirror left
after the actor has used the mirrors up. The wide angle lens.

The scene requires the release of several thousand gallons
of siphoned sea water. De-commissioned jet engines
fill the sails on action. It will run 15 on-screen seconds.

There's a delicacy born of dangerous
moments the producers are desperate to capture.

View playback. The lead's on-deck comportment
is casual, loaded with unrelinquished energies
cocked in slumped shoulders and languid, gorilla-like arms.

Tenderness confines its gestures to near misses, the use
of violence must always appear a life-saving measure.

Last looks. Final touches. An air horn blows.
The extras are miming. As the rubber saber
strikes my arm I'll react like it's cleaved to bone.

Which has less to do with feeling pain
than understanding timing. Apply glycerine tear.

. In the background all the British sailors
are Americans, all of the French are Mexicans.
Esta muy contento d'estai. Return to the dailies.

Now, when I'm alone I often act
as though someone else were watching.

Each take costs fifty grand. And the extras
continue to disappear, every time they leave
the picture frame. Cut. Cut. Camera reload.

They are about to roll again. Pretend. Be unreal.
Be more real than I have ever imagined.

THE BURIED

Catherine Graham

> *In a shallow grave of sand,*
> *done up to the nines*
> *in a huge flowery chiffon dress*
> *stretched out like a sail*
> *on a beach in the Hebrides,*
> *pecked to pieces by birds.*
> >   —Tilda Swinton

The breeze soothes the summer's
burning as it lifts off
the lake, but the hot
sand holds the white heat,
so we burrow our toes to find
the cooling. Bury me
in a shallow grave of sand.

I lie back and you shovel
beach over my pale
body. I let the itch of it
enter me. It's as if a thousand
insects have taken free reign
and clothed me in their stings. I am
dressed up to the nines

now, a level
away from all that I once knew.
A head. But when I close
my eyes I become
the buried.
A cloud passes over

in a huge flowery chiffon dress

and the sand is the smell
of my new skin. The grainy
case of my lungs pumps
through homes of crabs.
I am the sound
of the underneath
stretched out like a sail

in a photograph. I am pure
verb going nowhere.
Even the wind
can't move
me. The sand bars my body
from the water's rise
on a beach in the Hebrides

where time is carved back,
landlocked to the hours
of sand that has
no hours, only bones.
I'm not afraid
of your leaving; I'm only afraid of being
pecked to pieces by birds.

Daniel Day Lewis On Why He Left the Stage

Nathan Mader

A poisoned prop won't properly kill you
unless you've got a self-inflicted mind
and enough prep-time to think it through.
I'm a student of the method not a mime
constricted by the script. I get into it.
If you haven't noticed that I'm not here,
maybe I'm not making myself clear:
to be self-evident you must intuit
the dancer in the dance, become a victim
of another's circumstance. So don't ask
me who I met out on the grief-stricken
battlements and force me to unmask
this recollection. It wasn't my father's
ghost I fled but my self-reflection.

Upon Meeting Owen Wilson in a Grocery Store Where Almost Everything was Organic and All I Really Wanted was a Diet Coke (And Maybe a Mars Bar)

Shelley A. Leedahl

Paia, Maui. Last time I ever went anywhere with my family. We were shattering. We were down to the freakin' dregs.

Owen? Buying coffee. He looked at me and I glanced at him, then faster than you can spell *goofy blond celebrity* it was over. I followed him out the door and down a sandy lane for a time, not knowing why I'd bother, or what I might say if he suddenly turned and wondered why a middle-aged woman with sun-dried hair and flip-flops was simultaneously trailing him and wiping the sadness from her eyes with a "Hang Loose" beach towel.

My husband, our newly-adult kids: we got suited up like astronauts in neoprene and helmets and tore down the Haleakala volcano on sturdy bikes. We surfed. We snorkelled with turtles and the depths were like the moon. We drank so much on New Year's Eve we didn't make midnight. Cyndi Lauper sat behind us on the plane, and KC (of the Sunshine band) tossed back cool ones in the same bar as us. We devoured far too many of those fruity drinks that taste like sunshine and make you believe happiness is as easy to find as a white sand beach. I'd have drunk more had I known it'd be the last of us, forever and amen.

Owen Wilson? Looked like a friendly puppy. All I wanted from that particular hour was a Diet Coke and a solid hit of chocolate. Of course there's a lot more to it. Always is.

CAMEO APPEARANCE

Charles Simic

I had a small, nonspeaking part
In a bloody epic. I was one of the
Bombed and fleeing humanity.
In the distance our great leader
Crowed like a rooster from a balcony.
Or was it a great actor
Impersonating our great leader?

That's me there, I said to the kiddies.
I'm squeezed between the man
With two bandaged hands raised
And the old woman with her mouth open
As if she were showing us a tooth

That hurts badly. The hundred times
I rewound the tape, not once
Could they catch sight of me
In that huge gray crowd,
That was like any other gray crowd.

Trot off to bed, I said finally.
I know I was there. One take
Is all they had time for.
We ran, and the planes grazed our hair,
And then they were no more
As we stood dazed in the burning city,
But, of course, they didn't film that.

DIRECTORS, CHOREOGRAPHERS, CRITICS, AND WANNABES

SIGHT AND SOUND

Todd Swift

I read of films to know which films to see.
I rarely, if ever, refer to them as *movies*.

I prefer to rent DVDs. They carry so much extra
in the way of features; we enjoy the trailers more

than the main content: because the high-octane editing
compressing action, from choicest parts, is like *poetry*.

FIVE SILENT FILMS, POSTED TO YOUTUBE, WITH FRENCH SUBTITLES

rob mclennan

1.

only necessary we approach. requires sparseness, words. made up forgetfulness. across the island. as if to say her willingness a gap, her templed fore. or burned away, a birdsong. knows. a telephone will no longer make you immortal.

2.

what no longer means. an unlocked clarity of original sin. to be is not in itself happy or sad. the eye of strangers ventured, gained. a ghost of the water enters sunset. umbilical, somehow, attached.

3.

a stranger, air-conditioned. faith is willed attention, arming. the last pursuit of discourse, a piety provides. snow & rain in sequence fall at different rates. below ravines, each thinking is selected.

4.

cut out of roaring. autobiography, a wonderous position. thin syllables of knives. arsenic & talent, for the obvious. a blue-black love affair, a red prick spindle. sex & death, but only one an angel. line of honey you can't help but step upon.

5.

speak of the distill. the hard column, gradually, out. what actively
pursues, a templum carved out of a converse. named for pain,
small twitchy noises. mad, discovered, spinal. motions of flesh &
dawn akin to darkest rose. it opens.

In Memoriam Stan Brakhage (1933-2003)

Phil Hall

There is a library of strangers in Dublin
Kraków Iqaluit Constantinople Petticoat Junction
I have borrowed two silences from—the best sleep of my life
& light moving in a Stan Brakhage film

far away at home at last
I could not be reached breached or dissuaded
I slept forever & took forever to wake up & when I did
there goes your mime teacher all in white

light was archeologizing a patchwork quilt on a bed
dusting each snag as if there were no budget constraints
the approach of the children & the long-eared goat
was a Latin declension enacted

there is a library of strangers in Dublin
the Troy-warrens of its archives boustrophedonic
silence stoops to eyeball each shard & tag it
light tests its white hands against walls in the air

(distracted indifference from the old goat & the children)

HEARING PAN

Craig Poile

> *So the way we did it was this: he'd work out the steps*
> *with me—the Continental or whatever—then, having*
> *played Ginger to Fred, I would then go off, the dance*
> *all ready in my mind and then be Fred to Ginger.*
> —Hermes Pan

Weeks before film sees light
The two men polish the dance to routine.
Cheek-to-cheek, they rehearse until late,

Cobbling the steps she'll dance in, tighten
Each arc for an absent gown's sweep.
Stumbling in on Fred and Pan, the crew would lighten

Their shock with a joke, shout "sorry" and keep
Backing away from those queer, uncostumed poses:
Pan bent like a starlet, but his time came cheap.

When light pours on the stage, the camera closes
In to show he holds her no closer than Pan,
A space they cradle, a bright egg of ache, that loses

Nothing in translation as she falls upon
His circling arm, braced for a man's weight,
Her eyes catching the violet ebb of her spin.

Their passage leaves a limelight rub, a trace of what
Compelled them, in the grain of the late-late show
That watching shades drink in, down to the last watt.

His foot sounds are dubbed in later, so

You're seeing Ginger, but hearing Pan,
A dark, cunning rap that grounds her glow.

Like wings that lighten the feet, it happens,
And we can't put off the tap-tap invitation
To step onto the dark, empty floor and begin.

Part dazzle, part thievery, the carnal imitation
Of pale feathers blooming, the stiff collar pointed,
Or black silk, wetted to a "barely there" sensation.

For us no sleight of sound and light, instead
The sight and warmth of the chosen mate,
Dancing, duplicitous: a little Ginger, a little Fred.

His Domestic Pleasures Song

Ken Babstock

Flash-fried perogies. Wink. Antonioni.
Kurosawa. Cryptic crosswords. Kimchee.
Nights of Cabiria, Roma, Amarcord.
Out of the blue, your bathrobe doing it best Red
Sea, of its own accord. Finger paints.
Borage flowers fossilized in the ice tray.
At the business end of *War and Peace*,
getting the condensed version, in a glance.
Cat puke. Haircuts. *The Verve Collection.*
Muffins before the bananas rot. A rooftop garden.
Private language for misery, nothingness, joy,
acrimony. A list of names for a boy.
Coached to notice when mock orange is in bloom.
Left alone. But breath-sounds from the other room.

PROJECTOR

Elizabeth Ross

Night slides across dirty bus windows. Funny how my reflection doesn't move—face pale in the glass, blurred into two. Bench seat at the back, knees to my chest. Balled-up gum wrappers bounce as the bus swings to the edge of the street. I climb the hill in the cluttered dark, cut through the orchard behind the church, duck beneath spider webs and apples.

Dad warned me about characters here. I kick a beer can through the grass. The girl from *Mad Love* is still playing in my head. She's stopped at the convenience store for a pop, sits shotgun in her boyfriend's convertible, sips from a white straw. Strange shadows glide across the car's chrome grill. Her boyfriend admires her cheeks as her bare fingernails pinch the straw next to her lips.

He never tires of her, drives her to every breezy situation— deserted beaches, country roads—because she's beautiful and grateful, because her mouth is always on his neck, because she's running from parents who don't understand her.

She can see me. She followed me home from the theatre. Now I pass her and her boyfriend lying in the uncut grass beneath the largest tree. The girl rests her head on his tanned chest, his flannel shirt soft around her shoulders. Her jeans rolled up beneath his head, money for motels and hamburgers squished in the back pocket.

We both know how it ends. Her background will come into focus and she'll blur into pills, then shrinks, then hospitals. It's not that she wants to die. It's that cutting close to the negative is good therapy. He'll love her more strapped to the gurney, breasts curved beneath the paper blanket, and she'll be able to love herself. The trick is the control. The moon unspools reels of light. I let the right amount in on the scene.

LA POULETTE GRISE

Mitchell Parry

for Megan Ducker

La poulette grise *virtually defines 'moving pictures'*
while actually containing no movement at all.
                    —Peter Rist

1.
C'est la poulette grise
Qui pond dans l'église

Which came first—the egg
or the pearl-white clutch of stars?
Both are holy, if not sacred; close
as we can get to origin and endings.
The barred-rock nestles in the coop,
dreams egg, dreams chick. My mother
sang *Lula lula lula lula bye-bye*
and sleep pulsed behind my eyes.
Dad flicked off the light, closed
the door. Downstairs the living
room throbbed cathode blue.

2.
C'est la poulette noire
Qui pond dans l'armoire

Consider poor Zeno of Elea, who reclines
in the sun and considers. The black hen,
for example: she is either where she is
or where she isn't—in the cupboard
or not. Or an arrow, he thinks: it arcs from here
to there and holds each place between. A world
of fragments, say, or cells. Each moment

in the arrow's flight dissolves into the next.
Movement is impossible. Zeno crows
over his theory, his clever mind. Hen drops
to the ground, a flubbed shot, all fletching
and flap. She pecks at his sandal: *I refute it
thus.*

3.
*C'est la poulette jaune
Qui pond dans les aulnes*

Hay-stepping high-stepper, out
on a limb in that yellow dress
and your fiddle-dee-dee. Trace
your minuet and bow to your partner,
a reel and a jig—you're streaming
joy, petticoats and bloomers and your
heel-toe heel-toe stomping chips
from the floorboards, dust from
the hay loft. Even in lamplight
you are golden, auroral in a jig
and a reel. Two three four
in the morning til you dance
yourself out and doze against me
all the way home, sickle moon
and a dusting of galaxies astral
above our patchwork valley.

4.
*C'est la poulette blanche
Qui pond dans les branches*

In the dark of his studio McLaren
draws another hen & sighs. Another
hen, an egg. What is it
with these fucking birds? he thinks.
Cruel eyes & a brain you could hold
in a teaspoon. Fair enough, but then
the light that limns the barred-rock's cheeks,

or the plump chuffed rump of the white hen
& he's in love again with their sprightly
dancing trot, their rubber wattles & combs.
Given the chance, who wouldn't curl beneath
their brooding wings just once, if only
for a night? Roll the camera. He erases
the drawing, sketches another hen, another
egg. He'll be at this 'til cock-crow.

5.
C'est la poulette brune
Qui pond dans la lune

Sunset weaves a bolt of sky & cloud.
Venus rises in the west & hangs
at tree-height, or seems to. Sky's curve
is an illusion: constellations form, dissolve
into stars behind stars, a kind of mist,
a dusting. Their movement an illusion, too.
By which I mean they are always with us—
the Earth ball rolls in its track, the sun,
the moon. We see as best we can. We close
our eyes & go to sleep; we wake & do it all
again. One night the crescent moon
will scoop us up & cradle us as far as the stars.

GERALDINE

David Donnell

                              The critics didn't
think she was very good in Alan Rudolph's *Welcome to L.A.*
but I thought she
                     was fabulous, she was moody & beautiful
& angsty & I thought the single nude scene was stark &
isolated & in good taste. Taste is everything,
they say, taste is important. Somebody in London
said that a long time ago; and somebody in New York said,
Well, yes, but taste is a matter of taste. I'm glad
that George Santayana didn't become a language philosopher.
He was too intelligent, too interested in the world, too full of
exuberant spirits. Salubrious. Celerity. The wages for bad
writing like some recent Updike—well up you too & up u2—are
obscurity. He's definitely obscure in my living room. And the
salary for intelligence is love. OK. We're agreed on this.
The salary for intelligence is love. My mother used to love
long graceful stalks of celery fresh from the cold water tap
with just a touch of salt & stuffed with pimento cream cheese.
Sounds cheesy to you? Well, that's you, she was divine,
she was just simply a gorgeous woman,
and she loved it. Also sandwiches made with fresh whole wheat
bread lightly buttered & gently packed with sliced green olives.
She was interesting, more beautiful perhaps than that girl
in *Welcome to L.A.* but not angsty. And generally speaking, she
didn't do nude scenes.

CUKALORIS

Jason Guriel

> *Whatever is used to cast a shadow*
> *on something in a shot is known*
> *as a cukaloris. Why? I don't know.*
> —Roger Ebert

It lives
in the shadow
of the shadow
it gives
birth to.
We champion
the chiaroscuro,
not the grid
(placed before the light)
that garters
a starlet's thigh
with fishnet.
We praise
the shadow puppet,
not the naked
knot of fingers
that popped it
out without
the help of
women's hips.
It's not the moon
we want
it's the eclipse.

IN THE FILMS OF MICHAEL HANEKE

Mat Laporte

after Robert Creeley

He who laughs last
laughs first, this is how
a self constructs a self
through acts of blindness

through lonely winters
haranguing
the ice laden porch
with steeltoe dreams.

In a movie by Michael
Haneke, people stare
offscreen towards, god knows,
their incommunicable

steeltoed dreams of
losing themselves?
If only, they weren't
in a movie of Michael Haneke's

they would proceed,
as I do, one cold night
after another, by
wiggling their toes.

Claude Jutra's Note

gillian harding-russell

He gave up the dregs of his mind
                    for his soul, his soul
                protesting, 'this is my body—incredible
                but true': I am Claude Jutra,

let the world know.

Thoughts disoriented,
        out of sync, disposed of
            conveniently—*where there's will, there's a way*
                the self
        rising out of a carcass of brain.

A friend now speculates, he may not have had it at all—the dreaded
    Alzheimer's; when he stopped making films,
        he fed the squirrels more ...

            (red paisley squiggles on grass)

    Increasingly depressed, wanting

                a change, the silence

                    between frames.

The St. Lawrence mottled in grey ripples   brown sparkles
        like TV static, the perfect place
                            to drop everything

            amorphous

looking for a new shape.

But:
his films the preview, he knew: Mon Oncle Antoine (himself)

dragging himself (his corpse)

across the snow (tracks

obliterating tracks): the double signature
'me but not me.' Himself giving himself

a chance   to explore crystal flakes

sharp-angled   interstices

of the universe in galactic formation

at zero time.

SOUVENIR

Jeramy Dodds

Which is French for 'beneath veneer'
this title or my marriage? To remember
is to become a card-carrying member
of the past for as long as it takes to re-elect
your mistakes. Don't forget to remember,
dreamboat, change is a painful way to stay
the same. My recalled Renault explodes
past the glass factory. My remedial French class
is full of expats wearing cravats. My brain
missed the casting call for *Total Recall*.
John Bobbit was remembered, but to titillate the past
is disastrous. Mechanics now know Cannes is where
the undead weekend. Remember *Back to the Future*
when a death drive could repair your sweet ride?
My bit part in *Memento* flopped on the floor
of the editor's abattoir. My Renault's
at the factory being fitted for a Palme D'or.
Which is French for: I'm getting back to
getting back into you, by Parkour
atop ruins, hurtling dunes,
a rattlesnake skin
my windbreak

EXCERPTS FROM THE FUTURE MEMOIRS OF ROGER EBERT

Jacob McArthur Mooney

I was born with everything I needed.

I watched films for forty years and was fattened in Chicago.

I wrote down my thoughts.
My thoughts were thumbs.

I had a taste for vodka. This uninhibited me.
I leaned out an oval window and was caked in inhibitions.

I lost my best friend. I don't know where he went.

I grew famous. The spit in my cheeks turned to poison,

and my jaw grew tiny lumps. I shaved it smooth
and promised to never speak again. I became a political mystic.

I shook a tall man's hand and he pocketed my fingers.
I moved to Mogadishu and wrote recipes on tanks.

I jumped a barricade, but my feet stayed buoyed to the concrete.
I took a job making up the names of foreign leaders.

I rolled out of bed. My skin stayed folded in the sheets.
I developed a new theory of photography.

I adopted a child.
The only meat he would eat was the flesh on my back.

I asked my wife to draw my bath. The bath dissolved my bones
and sucked them down the sewer.
                            I became an author
of whimsical children's novellas.

One day, I blew away into the ocean. Amoeba mated in my hair.
I ceased to exist. I anthologized myself.

THE PARTICULAR MELON

Nick Thran

Walid was making a film about a particular
honeydew melon. *This* melon, he said,
pointing to the table littered with back issues

of *The Economist*, a BlackBerry Pearl, assorted
suspiciously pigmented utensils, and the melon
which lolled back and forth as their knees hit the table.

Why *this* melon? Frank asked. He was curious.
He was over-caffeinated. And why a film? Surely
this has something to do with the fruit trade

outside Lanzhou, the nefarious laws imposed
upon the disenfranchised? No, Walid said.
Let me stop you right there. I mean *this*

particular melon; which bears the fruit of a

singular summer. With its case like the skull
of a human being. Handled as quickly

by the hands of the pickers and transporters
as by the hands of the grocers, then cradled home
up two flights of stairs by my mother, lighting

the back end of her recurring shoulder injury;
she, the first female underground boxer
out of Pennsylvania in the 1960's. Wait, Frank said.

So this is a film about boxing? Barriers?
A blow-by-blow account of your mother's rise
to the rings of New York City? The melon

as a symbol of motherly love, a warrior's prowess?
The flesh of the fruit a symbol of memory,
of the toll the blows took over the years. How,

having forgotten the details of her past, she remains
a scooped out shell of her former self, until the seed
of familial love and artistic direction is planted by

your camera lens, and the world sees her as she was,
anew? Wow, Walid said. You've had a lot of coffee.
Please let me finish, Frank said. I want to understand *this*

particular melon, and perhaps the clerk, brunette,
late teens, holding it above her head, and calling
for a price check while the rest of the line

grows anxious and impatient. Holding it steadily
while your mother looks on, admiring her strength
and thinking, perhaps, that she is seeing the torch

being passed from one generation of boxers
to the next, as sentimental and distractedly triumphant
a moment as she has ever known in the ring,

spitting blood into her bucket while the fat cats

in the front row spill vodka tonics on their leather shoes.
Then, Walid said, we will funnel the chords of a song

through the air between her missing teeth.
Something distinct, Frank said. Yes, Walid said,
something fresh off the heels of the blues.

SCARY MOVIES, THRILLERS, HORROR FLICKS AND FILM NOIR

Werewolf Movies

Margaret Atwood

Men who imagine themselves covered with fur and sprouting
fangs, why do they do that? Padding among wet
moonstruck treetrunks crouched on all fours, sniffing
the mulch of sodden leaves, or knuckling
their brambly way, arms dangling like outsized
pajamas, hair all over them, noses and lips
sucked back into their faces, nothing left of their kindly
smiles but yellow eyes and a muzzle. This gives them
pleasure, they think they'd be
more animal. Could then freely growl, and tackle
women carrying groceries, opening
their doors with keys. Freedom would be
bared ankles, the din of tearing: rubber, cloth,
whatever. Getting down to basics. Peel, they say
to strippers, meaning: take off the skin.
A guzzle of flesh
dogfood, ears in the bowl. But
no animal does that: couple and kill,
or kill first: rip up its egg, its future.
No animal eats its mate's throat, except
spiders and certain insects, when it's the protein
male who's gobbled. Why do they have this dream then?
Dress-ups for boys, some last escape
from having to be lawyers? Or a
rebellion against the mute
resistance of objects: reproach of the
pillowcase big with pillow, the tea-
cosy swollen with its warm
pot, not soft as it looks but hard
as it feels, round tummies of saved string in the top
drawer tethering them down. What joy, to smash the

tyranny of the doorknob, sink your teeth
into the inert defiant eiderdown with matching
spring-print queensized sheets and listen to her
scream. Surrender.

NOSFERATU

Vanessa Moeller

I find the rabbit-hearted beauty
by echolocation, by speaking rust
off my voice and into the dark.
Each syllable is outline—
thigh, wrist, nape,
deep chalice of clavicle.

I disremember how light ribbons
through dust motes, how warmth
feels inside my flesh
and each thick, musty breath
is the droning taste of forever.

But vulnerabilities exist—stakes and
sunlight may come. Humans
have limited revulsion,
only love predators
that would never truly prey on them.

BRIDE OF FRANKENSTEIN

Alex Boyd

These discs are the best use for technology,
forget sending businessmen to England
in four hours, they'll just want to go in three.
Here's how it works: the disc spins,
and for every little Boris there's a little Bride
deep in the silver, somewhere under
your reflection, the worry lines on your brow.
They meet and spin and the film starts to play.
So what if Lon Chaney is a plump Wolf Man,
or the body count just isn't all that high.
In the days before quantity meant more,
murdering a few people made you evil.
And so what if the Lugosi Dracula is staked
off camera, heads turning—you don't need
to see every bloody thing, now do you.
Again the villagers are back with torches,
tearing down signs all over town,
Assistant needed: must be hunchbacked,
have two years experience pulling levers.
Boris doesn't scare me—I'm taking him
to stand there, right at the entrance
where the world pours thickly into my dreams,
his instructions: smash all the unhappiness.

King Kong Meets Wallace Stevens

Michael Ondaatje

Take two photographs—
Wallace Stevens and King Kong
(Is it significant that I eat bananas as I write this?)

Stevens is portly, benign, a white brush cut
striped tie. Businessman but
for the dark thick hands, the naked brain
the thought in him.

Kong is staggering
lost in New York streets again
a spawn of annoyed cars at his toes.
The mind is nowhere.
Fingers are plastic, electric under the skin.
He's at the call of Metro-Goldwyn-Mayer.

Meanwhile W.S. in his suit
is thinking chaos is thinking fences.
In his head—the seeds of fresh pain
his exorcising,
the bellow of locked blood.

The hands drain from his jacket,
pose in the murderer's shadow.

MONSTER (GODZILLA)

Sachiko Murakami

No one loves a beast of a man in the body of a beast
who, at Hollywood parties, lurks in the kitchen, gulping punch,
spits sunflower seeds when a pretty girl forces him to speak,
leaves on a motorcycle. Looks silly hunched over it.

This is a fact, his life without love.

When Donne wrote *No man is an island*
Godzilla wasn't real yet, slept in the Pacific
until the bomb shook its little boy's fist
and he wandered into the studio.

We fear most that he might snap,
scoop up virgins and carry them off to Asia
where, unable to secure employment,
they'd be forced into arranged marriages.
After finding diaries with hearts looped
around the letter G, concerned parents
hand their daughters to psychiatrists, who diagnose
Godzillamania. They've pills for it.

This is a fact, the threat of him.

Downtown, night. Lightning strikes once or twice
to reveal his bestial face. He'd reflect
on his mission if the script said more than
SCENE 25. STORM. LIGHTNING STRIKES
ONCE OR TWICE. GODZILLA
MELTS GLASS TOWERS WITH
APOPLECTIC BREATH.

This is a fact, his imagined life.

And at his feet, a grocery list
rain-stuck to a bus shelter. In it,
virgins huddle and share a rosary.

Virgins are the first facts. Women are secondary.

He's suspect of the film's tricks,
forgets sometimes he's larger than life.
Can't tell when the film stops rolling
and accidentally squashes extras.
The studio uses the footage. Audiences gobble it up.
Shot out of scale, next to Godzilla
the victims seem as big as thimbles, and as useful.

BATMAN

Kelsey Mills

It's not the noises in the night that they're afraid of,
It's the triumph of the inner demon
Hidden in the concealed weapon.

And you?

Deep down, *every one*
Is Two Face.
Deep down, *every one*
Is the Joker.
We want to make the world laugh
And watch the world burn
On morality's silver edge.

If the cowl only hides a riddle
And the crusade is retribution
With flowing fabric,
The shots are not from guns
But from the blood on your hands.

FILM NOIR

Carmine Starnino

We were agents sifting intelligence from chatter
when static gave up the heartbeat.
                                 On screen,
a motion picture of interstellar fuzz, or fizzing

phosphorescence, shaken, full of direction.
We watched sleeper cells chase each other in dream-paced
hide and seek, dust to dust,
                                 until a rorschachwise drift
came clean, until a shape, cross-examined,
snitched.
                 Across from us, a suspect with a changing story.
Let's go through it one more time, we sighed.
"Hand and wrist!" he suddenly confessed.
Adrenaline pumping, we held out for the rest.

SCARY MOVIES

Kim Addonizio

Today the cloud shapes are terrifying,
and I keep expecting some enormous
black-and-white B-movie Cyclops
to appear at the edge of the horizon,

to come striding over the ocean
and drag me from my kitchen
to the deep cave that flickered
into my young brain one Saturday

at the Baronet Theater where I sat helpless
between my older brothers, pumped up
on candy and horror—that cave,
the litter of human bones

gnawed on and flung toward the entrance,
I can smell their stench as clearly
as the bacon fat from breakfast. This
is how it feels to lose it—

not sanity, I mean, but whatever it is
that helps you get up in the morning
and actually leave the house
on those days when it seems like death

in his brown uniform
is cruising his panel truck
of packages through your neighborhood.
I think of a friend's voice

on her answering machine—
Hi, I'm not here—
the morning of her funeral,
the calls filling up the tape

and the mail still arriving,
and I feel as afraid as I was
after all those vampire movies
when I'd come home and lie awake

all night, rigid in my bed,
unable to get up
even to pee because the undead
were waiting underneath it;

if I so much as stuck a bare
foot out there in the unprotected air
they'd grab me by the ankle and pull me
under. And my parents said there was

nothing there, when I was older
I would know better, and now
they're dead, and I'm older,
and I know better.

MOVIE MONSTER

Blaise Moritz

Looking at the monster projected on the screen,
a papier-mâché model in harmony with the cardboard
kingdom over which it exercises a playful reign of terror,
I think how the black and white makes cohesive
this fantasy which must in the studio have looked patchwork
and ill-coloured, how the limitations of the medium
contribute to the enduring power of these images.
To me, they're not yesterday's crap, pre-stop motion, pre-CGI,
but a vision, integral and necessarily equal to any
subsequent vision, regardless of technical advances,
realized, with that acceptance of materials that defines
the artist, by a sci-fi auteur, recognized in these latter days,
but only as a 'pioneer'. All cry for something beyond the modern,
something novel and alien, and have framed this criterion for
their hope:
that the unreal should be indistinguishable from the real.
And what would the auteur think were he equipped
with the tools of our contemporary filmmakers, then asked
to sit through his dated masterpiece; mightn't he agree
with the genre fans that this movie is put to shame
by later effects, which reframe his bold strokes as failed graspings.
And would he too re-make them, endlessly regenerating
his monsters and explosions in state-of-the-art manner,
leaving me alone to face dismissal as sentimental, contrarian
for my insistent love of his original images, in their imperfections
more perfect than the wonders of tomorrow? I've read
that in the climactic scenes, the monster's joyous rampage,
the creature's beautiful fluidity was achieved
using stand-ins, the usual match-box towers replicated at dollhouse
scale, the place of the menacing dwarf model taken

by a man in a rubber costume. Great fun it must have been,
amok amidst that town to be destroyed. What motivation
was the actor given? *You are lost in a strange and hostile place.*
You must erase this world if you are to build your own.
Got it. Roll 'em, and I'll start smashing.

SCREENPLAY BY KING

Dave Margoshes

The dream—*the nightmare!*—unfolds
like a Stephen King movie, quietly, building
suspense, with its own logic. There are
small creatures, horrible, the product
of special effects, and once they attach
themselves they drain the life from you
and they can't be detached, become
your Siamese twin. What wakes you
is the sound of screaming, not your own
but one of the characters, a young woman
attacked in her tub. The creature is no bigger
than a leech at first, but grows quickly,
the size of a kitten, a child, and then
the woman appears to be embracing
a younger version of the actress playing
her role, then making love with a mirror,
and all the while she is screaming
to be separated from herself. When you
do finally awake you shake your head
with the usual disbelief, it was so real,
you could see every detail, it really *was*
like a movie, the characters and storyline
all unknown to you, based on a novel
you've never read. You're shaken, have
a glass of water and sit on the edge of the bed
trying to think of something else, anything
to get the last wisps of dream out of your head,
not the screaming so much as the certainty
that you too are permanently attached
to yourself.

New Rats

Emily Schultz

I relate to the rats, the rats that run like a river,
because I have known rats.

Those of alley eateries, now and then thieving
their way into my closets.

They've scrambled among winter boots, soiled
pages of old diaries.

In this version, they hatch from black caskets
packed solid with earth.

Even evil closes its eyes, sleeps, must sleep
in the ground where it was born.

Carried by river, this cargo eats grown men
in a solitary night.

This ship bumps to shore, brown rats rise from water,
bubbling, flooding the city.

As if a phantom is divided among a thousand incurrent
beasts, each lugs disease.

And in our own lives, how often did we avoid moving closer,
gazing into the coffins of relatives?

The bald man with long fingernails. The dirt.
And vermin.

Inside inexplicably, like necrophagous flies.
These rats.

They step over one another on supper tables,
tombs, church steps.

Colliding ghosts on ground level. The genetic similitude
of a thing

that sees by sonar, flies blind, sleeps upside-down,
and a thing

that scratches the backs of cabinets, nibbles the night,
sees with its teeth.

Fifty years before I was born, the original, *eine symphonie des grauens*.

JAMES BOND CONSIDERS RETIREMENT

Paula Jane Remlinger

> *I'll buy you a delicatessen.*
> —Ernst Blofeld, villain, *For Your Eyes Only* (1981)

For a moment Bond considers
trading the trench coat for an apron ripe
with salami spice, mustard stretched thin
as winter sun, the everyday clatter.

He thinks of kissing Moneypenny
who hungered so long, wanting him like
smoked ham wants a hint of Dijon. He wonders
what it would be like to stop minding

his Ms and Qs, the pens that shoot
but don't write, women and cars
likely to blow without warning.
His back hurts these days, harder to slalom,
leap from a plane, wrestle sharks
or swarthy men without wrinkling

his tuxedo, harder to make love underwater,
needing the oxygen tank more often
than not, harder to drink those damn
martinis, liver shrivelled like a rancid olive.

Everything harder.
(Almost everything.)

For a moment you think Bond hesitates—
he hovers, then tips the chopper politely
like a gentleman's hat and you plummet
revenge green as dill on the tip of your tongue.

INDELIBLE IMAGES

FRONTIER, IN CINECOLOR

George Amabile

Out there among mesas and arroyos,
chollas, saguaro and prickly pear,
a flatbed wagon leaves a trail
of dust on the road out of town.

The steam locomotive, black
with gold trim, dragging its chain
of chuffs and clanks down Main Street,
rattles the gilt-lettered windows

of the shops. Sometimes a drifter
hops off a freight-car, drops
a few silver dollars at the Saloon,
or Madame Heidi's Desert Rose

Emporium. He'll be seen at the Bank,
the Post Office, the General Store.
But it won't be long before his eyes
turn, toward the mountains, and the sea.

SLOW MOTION

Lillian Necakov

after Jean Vigo's Zero de Conduite, *1933*

Here's the thing
I was going through some movie stills
and I found one, of the final shot
of a film I saw at least a decade before I ever met you

four boys climbing the roof of the school house
a victorious gang of rebels soaring up to the heavens
with nothing on their minds
arms raised like Esther Williams about to dive into a pool
of diamonds and feathers

years before I had known your voice, I heard it
in slow-motion
during the same film on a Friday morning
with snow coming in on northern wings
spilling its contents down on us
thousands of tiny frozen finger nails
on our landscape
reminding us of the most important scene
when the boys rip open a room full of pillows
and find a silent grace in their flowering.

CATCH AND RELEASE

Ian LeTourneau

Its glide was perceptible. Then it lodged,
stuck. Submerged in a silent film, my mind

treading celluloid. Around the table,

conversation carried on, muted. I fumbled
with the ill-fitting key of epiphany. I am

choking on a fish bone. Should have waved

my hands, thumped the table; instead I tensed
up, calmly analyzing, urging reversal.

Static permeated the room like the big screen

between reel changes. Then the mechanical
momentum of film clicking into place began

anew. On my plate, in a soup of mashed food,

a slender piece of evolution. My mind
gulping a few quick breaths to catch up.

ARTICLE OF FAITH

Adam Sol

David: coming home from a film today, my brain
so enmeshed in a close-up of an actor's mouth and teeth
that I almost walked into a bus, I thought of you.
Only you could make me love L.A.,
you with your electric beard.
Years ago we poured ablutions of Ethiopian beer
over the feet of the Buddha, you and I;
we climbed concrete to a beach bonfire;
we sneered at Trader Vic's like upright citizens,
and I want to tell you that I am no longer as lost as I was.
I know when I saw you last I was counting slips
and the numbers weren't good.
I want things more than I want to want them.
You, though, were steadfast like a priest.
You were true like the word tries to be true.
I read in the paper about a pilot who veered
his crashing plane into the waves
to save whomever he thought
lived in an empty farmhouse he could see from the cockpit.
We need our fictions. And look:
your California coast shimmers with promises,
with mists and frigates;
and I am in possession of a goodly heritage,
a dynasty of defiance with acrostic martyrologies.
And yet despite our bruised students,
despite our shaky foundations
and everything we know about everything we know,
I still have this vague, wiry
belief growing in me like a cactus,
like acacia clinging to the crumbling soil.
You know about this—it's you who taught me.
I'm writing to tell you, David, that I accept, I accept it all.

Let the idols of apathy be multiplied,
I will not take their names upon my lips.
I am hefting my ideologies—with all their incumbent clichés—
and I am carrying them to California.
My friend, amidst the shards of our deconstruction
I believe there grows a kind of manna.
I am writing my way West to celebrate some old lies with you.

Depression Pictures

Glen Downie

You never knew when the neighbours might break
into song. It's a pity they don't
make 'em like that anymore.
Back then, lots of folks just lived
for that ribbon of dreams.
Swimming women
unfolding
their legs into flowers.

FILM IN AN UNKNOWN TONGUE

A.F. Moritz

Bangkok.
The naked god of love,
adolescent, violet-colored, scarred,
in his stiletto boat
conveys two Caucasian women.
Skiffs careen in the wash.
Paintless huts.
Children on mossy doorsteps.

At the stone lions the boatman,
smoking agèd engine in his hand,
delivers them.
The stairs come from under water
and beneath climbing sandals
the slime of another world,
lips exchanging moisture in darkness.

Who is that whitewashed statue
cracked and peeling,
in a tuneless voice making impure proposals?
There is nothing in the human world
but women and that voice
seeking a living throat to speak it.

Nothing but women
and the sea swell at dusk:
the depths manifest in the surface,
bowels present in the skin
and its silk of light,
contentment in a motion as of hips,
a loose motion playing across

the day's rhythm,
a motion of breasts
molding eyes and hands.

Nothing but women and a vagrant light.

They are naked now
in the deserted garden
and their throats are pitchers.
Let us go down.
Nothing is moving now.
It is the freedom of which we dreamed.

O violation,
                beautiful youth,
once we were you.
Again now we feel that first anger
and the surprise of floating free.
Now in this palace of wood above the river
the plants tend themselves
and hope is the air.

Wine created the vessel
and the full vessel,
for someone to drink from it,
created man:
                even the man
who drinks from and refreshes
two Caucasian women
amid the gilding of cries and knives
and the cancer flowers.

Oz: A Tribute to Gerda Taro*

John Reibetanz

No going back to Kansas for this girl   Auntie Em
and the other aunts and uncles   already being
rounded up   and ushered into boxcars   no lion

or tin man to pull them out   no pail of tears to quench
flames sending scarecrows   up the chimneys   her filming done
two years before the movie shoot begins   her gravestone

will be carved by Giacometti   levelled by Nazis
and replaced with concrete   but she cares no more for stone
than for going back   to being Gerta Pohorylle

Polish typist   swept from Leipzig by the swastika's
twister   her yellow brick road   leading to Paris where
in place of ruby slippers   she clicks the shutter of

a Rollei   and learns to soar   beyond her typewriter's
clattering wings   the feather stroke of the aperture
outflying flight   lifting her into a self-made star

flash-lit like Garbo   shimmering with the magic art
of Taro Okamoto   mere dazzle until Spain
focuses her heart   on other refugees   bodies

hunkered in shelters and dugouts   spread unlullabied
on marble slabs   wide-open eyes   demanding she look
not at but through their lenses   over the rainbows of

their irises   above the chimney tops of Europe
to the pure rising   they dare to dream   and her snapshots
find it   not in the skies   but in their living bodies

amid the rubble of bombed Cordoba   children turn
a fallen beam into a see-saw   in defiance
of gravity and blackshirts   a blind musician floats

on the carpet   of his concertina's unfolding
notes   and two running soldiers lift into symmetry
a pas de deux   on the monochrome   where you'll find them

Photojournalist, b. Germany 1910, killed 1937 while covering the Spanish Civil War. Replacing her last name Pohorylle with Taro, she constructed her pseudonym to combine the glamour of Greta Garbo with the artistic credo of the painter and sculptor Taro Okamoto, who proclaimed that "art is magic" and that art should recognize no boundaries.

EMERALD CITY BLUES

Phoebe Tsang

> *for Kate Rogers*

Forty percent of the city is green!
Behind her the ziggurat-spine
of mountains was cascading
down to Kowloon Harbour where
a small girl posed for her photo
beside Bruce Lee—he'd been standing
so long in the midday sun
his skin had blackened to bronze.
I saw no plaque on his plinth,
he didn't need one.
No junks in the water, no more
red paper sails webbed like dragons' tails.

On the far shore, glass-eyed monoliths glared
behind a blue-grey curtain of smog.
The view from our sixteenth-floor
restaurant was clear, flecked
with treetops like clusters
of Swarovski crystals dyed
the colour of emeralds—
impressive, without the cost.

My hilltop-dwelling friend was happy
as a bird here; over lunch she sang
the praises of parks and hiking trails
backed by the verdant
vista unfurled at the window.
It was my first day in Hong Kong
and I was in love with the aerial view

I'd drifted down into just
hours ago, past mountains
lush as giant leaf-clad breasts.

That day, I hadn't yet journeyed to the glass
heart of the Emerald City and seen
Dorothy curtseying before a life-size statue
surrounded by souvenir shops.
Maybe it was the weather—forty degrees
on the boardwalk, sweating in my jeans—
even with my tinted glasses,
I couldn't make out a hint of green
through the poisoned mists.

It's been eighteen years since
I last saw my hometown
but now that I've crossed the Pacific
and docked in her harbour,
all I'd ask of the great Oz
is to take us back to the forest.

Instruments from Oz or Paranoid Indian

David Groulx

John Wayne is trying to kill me
he has a Winchester on his hip
Custer is hiding under my bed
with his saber in his hand
he'll cut me open
if I close my eyes

I haven't slept in years

Jesus is coming to civilize
me and make blue-eyed Indians
performing miracles
with gunpowder made out of wine
and land made out of small pox

the Sûreté du Québec are hiding
in my closet behind wire hangers and
boxes of pictures of my
grandmothers and grandfathers
my aunts and uncles
my father and mother

I've set up barricades at the closet doors

The Hudson Bay Company has been raiding my fridge
I can tell because all the boiled moose meat
and the half bottle of beer are gone
they went to the toilet
and used the last of the Charmin

The police take shots at me when no one
is looking

they point their pistols and wink
they are conspiring to kill me
drag me out to the outskirts of town
and leave me there to freeze to death

I called the media
they didn't believe me
told me I was paranoid and crazy
and I began to believe them

John

Jim Smith

In that dream, I fought John Wayne. It started with our fists and I was amazed by the look of surprise on his face just before his sledgehammer blow knocked me out. When I stood, the six-gun was hot in my hand, and as I raised it I heard a strange barking sound coming from his hand, bandaged as it was. Taking one in the shoulder, I fell and picked up the M-16 that lay there at hand. Firing from a prone position, I was able to see the pin he pulled from the thing he threw as I thought I'd winged him and after the smoke had cleared I could see him sitting at a console that mirrored the one where I sat, panting. Partway to the red button, both of our fingers halted, and he turned to me, and said well sonny I think I might just join you. I stood and walked toward him, wary and scared as hell. His handshake hurt as much as the first punch in the face he had given me as a child.

APOCALYPSE NOW

Patrick Warner

An insistent buzz, or vibration, like a screw
loose somewhere in the typewriter casing,
broke the silence compounding where I sat,
hands frozen above the ivory-coloured keys.
I found him upturned on the windowsill,
his black thready legs knitting a backdrop
of deciduous, but jungle-dense, foliage
and the brown river flecked with pleasure boats.
Disabled, he was the unexplored horizon,
turning blue, gasoline green and turquoise
as the paddle-shaped hair-clip turned him,
prompting a Brandoesque slur of consonants—
something about the mirror, the mirror.

WHAT WE REMEMBER

Jim Nason

There was calm and then
the iceberg. From above
we must have looked like two thousand
trembling candles. The dark was also shivering.
Some of us held hands, or drank
champagne. White rockets were sent to the sky.
We all knew what was coming.

The stern rose higher.
Everything not bolted down slid
across the floor. A propeller shaft, wide as a barn,
tall as a totem of twenty men, came out of the water.
Then her first note. The high-pitched tip, blue and frigid,
the luminous swell that rose from the deep. Cabin lights
like gleaming stars splashed across the sea.

THE WOMAN IN THE CARPET

Maxianne Berger

after Makhmalbaf's Gabbeh

when they rolled open
                    the knotted wool carpet
they found a woman
              her blue dress unravelling
brown hair long and loose
                  tangled with winds of the steppe
matted with the silt of river banks

the hand-spun fibres
                dyed in flowers and berries of the fields
feel coarse as the far hills
            slate peaks against a rippled sky

her eyes drawn open
             appear to focus
but she never could see
              the black-hooded rider
        approaching behind
                muddied boots smudging
        the grey mare's flanks

as he bears down on her

        her mouth contorts

there she remains

      always out of reach

OPEN

Lorri Neilsen Glenn

Your room unlocked those summer days
by the river. Cash, keys, a bottle of gin, loose silk
shirts, a watch, a well-thumbed collection
of short stories—all abandoned
like spilled spoons on the floor of a dream.

Wind in the afternoon lifting
the curtains, sails of ships,
Marilyn Monroe's white dress unfurling above
the subway vent, lives you wanted
to live, your lungs: everything

that fills, empties, fills again.
Sun in your eyes a pearl pried from a dark shell,
glinting inside your bones. And you,
the river, all the wet
hollows of the earth, opening.

Mon Chair

Weyman Chan

Air rising from a subway grate.
Angela Vickers falling for her dark-eyed
horse, twice removed and hitched to someone else.
Smoke-voiced Dark Angel in silver
cuffs   with riding crop

one raised brow can jump-start puberty or
flag an ambulance:
oh fashionable hysteron in vee-crotched
terminatrix get-up,
if you stalk cinema
to get at my juvenile heart,
then cinema will in turn make a douche of
cigarette-mouthed heel climbers. One Velvet Fog
or Hefeweissen at the Bear and Kilt will be enough to
slip me under the table of your gropey wit.

I'll cross-dress and one-leg any chair on any stage
for the next two centuries, just to feel
hard-boiled and with it.

You have the sway of Scarlett for Melanie's toy, without
the penitence of a dying socialite. There's no dark victory
when these colour-coded golden
hucksteresses pass us through
their age-appropriate circus folds—

still, there is the question of men
getting off on perpetual dyke distraction,
much like crunching mints to get at
the taste of their own breath.

Way to go, guys. Still feeding off
dynamite and vampishness
when Mommy's not around,
so which rival am I vying for?

From an obstetrical genie point-of-view,
Vanna spins vowels, Judy popped
pill-boxes, while *vain* and *wannabe*
slunk around.

Some ingénue catches air billowing over
her pleated knees, and it's truly
sweet, gullible enough to
take me for a ride. Like
wearing opera gloves
for the first time.

WHEN A FRIEND LENDS A POET MOVIES

Eleonore Schönmaier

for Nancy Creed

Like the gap in the wall behind
the filing cabinet that hides a tunnel
into John Malkovich's brain,
the door at the head of the poet's bed
leads directly into her control
centre: hum of green
lights, a large blue ball,
a red kneeling chair, a globe
of the upside down world
showing Oceania.

A sailor sleeps in the poet's bed
while she bounces on the blue
ball. Words scroll down the face
of her turquoise Apple.
With her mouse as guide, poems vanish
and her Apple plays movies.
When her sailor wakes up
she tells him: "You're not allowed
into my brain
without kissing me first."

BETTING ON THE HORSES

Lisa Pasold

You were betting on the horses at seven years old, choosing
the one that looked most like Black Beauty, pretending to be
Elizabeth Taylor in *National Velvet*—because that's the era you
wanted, her perfect violet eyes.

Though even at seven, you knew your own eyes were brown and
never would be violet.

That old film gave off such a feeling of sexual tension. You couldn't
figure them out, Elizabeth and tiny ex-jockey Mickey Rooney and
the horse. What's with teenage girls and horses?

You drew Cleopatra eyeliner under your eyes with magic marker.
How fast could you go? By the time you hit adolescence, you were
living in Scarborough and horses were the least of your worries.

Stormblue

Robyn Sarah

> *You're rich, and you want to be loved like a poor man.*
> *—Les enfants du paradis*

The way a woman loves a man
without money: for the holes
in his socks, for the tilt
of his eyebrows, for his voice
singing a song or murmuring
behind a door, for the fragrant
smoke of his pipe bluing the air
in the small old cozy cluttered room,
for his patched elbows, his
tweedy jackets from the Nearly New,
for the blind intelligence
of his body in love, for his hands,
quiet on the table, their dance
in the air when he speaks,
for the mole
on the back of his neck, for a few
old jokes that he likes to tell,
for his laugh,
for the way his hair sticks up
in the morning, for the cleft
in his chin, for a dimple
(seldom seen) in his left cheek,
for his dreams, and the light
that they put in his eyes
evenings of dreamy talk—

For the blue of his eyes
that she calls
his baby eyes

that grow stormblue
in anger at being loved
for the foolish things
she loves him for,
because they are all he has
to give her,
because he knows
that she knows
he will never
have more.

THE SEVENTH SEAL

Kirsteen MacLeod

Our path is green with rain
buttercups spill yellow, trees all
apple blossom, warbler call and flutter
strawberries glow like rubies in the grass

I linger at each new patch, red lips
and fingers, stark film images
still flickering black and white
in my head:

Last night, we watched those knights,
haunted by death, return from the Crusades.
They found respite in a sunny meadow,
bowls filled
with wild berries and milk

I taste the sweet-tart fruit, wonder why
I always play the gambolling squire,
protesting endings,
while you, the noble knight,
walk on with meditative, mile-eating steps

In Revelation, when the seal was broken,
there was silence in heaven for half an hour:

So if there is no god, only death,
can we at least lose our fear,
live simply, share small joys?

At this moment you return,
pour into my palm all you've collected—
berries spill over into the tangled blades
and we kneel, in pursuit

Hiroshima. Mon amour

Colin Morton

In this fallen world of ours we sometimes need to revisit the causes of our youth, just as we return on video to the films we lined up for outside theatres once. Without admitting it, we look for a shadow of the innocent person we were, perhaps even a glimmer of the person we held hands with across the armrest long after they became sweaty and cramped, reluctant to let go a moment too soon.

So that August, Hiroshima Day at the park's reflecting pool, I balanced a tea light on an origami boat and set it adrift beside the others, glancing idly about in case she too had taken it into her head to return years later to where we met.

I lie. That was the third August running I launched my hopes that way, and my glance was idle only because I had little hope left of seeing her. Our parting had been painful, and though we made a truce, I never put much faith in those promises to keep in touch. Years passed without so much as a phone call or email. But there she was kneeling at poolside, setting her own fragile craft adrift on an invisible current toward the far shore.

Her hair was shorter than in student days, but I recognized her instantly. Her eyes searched mine as keenly as ever when she asked if I meant to go with the peace group to the showing of *Hiroshima mon amour,* never a favourite of mine, she knew.

Of course, I answered, and feigned disappointment when the organizer announced the film had not arrived.

In its place: the war epic *Ran.* An inspired choice, we agreed afterward over coffee. We could think of none better to show the futility of war. The fall of kingdoms, wilful blindness, blindness inflicted by others. False love, lost causes, lost time. And the unforgettable moment, as palaces burned, when she reached over and after all those years took my hand.

FARGO IN FLOOD

Stephanie Bolster

I've never been to any of my favourite places
but I saw the film, that north American town
ensconced in snow. A pregnant woman stood
on a blood-flecked plain beside a car wreck,

pronounced a man dead. Now, like all those
grey roads in my sleep, Fargo's under water.
Minnows pass through open windows
of that upturned car, lodge in the dead

man's pockets. The current sways him as if
he were alive, in love. Somewhere, the actress
from the film stands by a river with her son,
that swelling within her on the movie screen now

actual. On another channel, Manitoba grows heavy,
towel darkening with spill. I dream
of ghostly birch immersed, roots nudging up.
Those women in the wreckage, seeking

photographs of children, will find
life's become a soggy matter in their hands,
no one's to blame. I wake to red
on threadbare sheets, another thin blue sky.

On the Beach

Louisa Howerow

The camera lens catches Ava running
Greg waiting on the pier, sun setting
between their lips, radioactive dust
pausing on its way to Melbourne where
everyone is trying to hold on,
planting gardens, believing the earth
still welcomes seeds. The navy captain writing
letters, buying gifts, as if his wife
and children were alive—maybe
they are, who knows. Drawn to miracles,
I sing Waltzing Matilda
to my six-foot rubber plant,
not because it's beautiful,
but because it's reaching
toward the ceiling, maybe through it,
like the momentum of empty arms
that don't listen to reason,
like the neighbour who blesses
the ringed turtle doves on the fire escape,
his mellow voice rising
and falling with their kooo-krooo.

A WAY TO PICTURE LOVE

Michael Oliver

I died
And it was like
The city late at night—
Like film noir when luck runs out.

But then
I heard wild footsteps
Racing after me—
And there you were, the girl I married.

Suddenly,
Beyond the tears, beyond the pain—
Like Jane and Tarzan in a 1930s movie—
We begin a bright new day by swimming naked underwater.

How can you fall asleep?

Tonja Gunvaldsen Klaassen

How can you fall asleep?
I resist the drift—separate cities wrought with gates

clanging shut. Rain: oxidized, electric,
falling. I admit it, I admit—demons, legion.

Your wet belt-buckle at the top of the heap,
Paris long behind us.

Tonight—flashes in the darkened theatre
between black and white—

horseshoes, hammers; yellow roses;
a young girl's pretty hands, examined

(the flat nail of your thumb thinking my wrists)
her insistence: now *choose.*

Our bicycles in rain over the train bridge, after *Toto le héros*
down Queen Street and 6th Avenue towards home. I'm lost,

can't follow you easily to sleep.
The screen door to the kitchen garden, latched—

a cross-hatch of darknesses in stove light.
Bee balm rising in the night

while I heat water for tea in a long-handled pot,
ladle it out.

I am in love's *wrong place*
in another hour, and another—

THE ROCKY HORROR LYRIC POEM

Eric Folsom

In the darkness of our strangest, stormy skulls,
With everyone's blonde hair slicked flat in the rain,
There's lightning and a pair of lips asking what strange
Might mean to us and the rest of society,
How it shapes the balance of people we know,
Or thought we knew—vampire lip gloss lordosis,
Sticky feather boas, grandfather clocks,
The rainbow slab crib of the conjuror's box.
Like finding a game of spin-the-bottle
With newly met teens when you're only twelve,
Like walking through the park in tight, ripped cut-offs
And feeling the eyes of men on your skin,
It's the party where costumes make puppets of people,
You clutch your beer bottle cause you can't trust the punch,
It's a Brandy Alexander in a dark biker bar,
A night time granite monument on hallucinogens.
Deliciously it dawns on you everyone's watching,
And old Frankie Coyote, the Monstre Sacré,
Turns back to a tree stump, then the pastor at church;
You wake with a start to the cool of your wetness,
Remember dream angels in stiff, frozen denim
Who shifted the sexual furniture while you slept,
So you fret in the glare of diurnal emissions
How skewed you might be and which way.
Shuffle the cards of furious confusion,
Smear them face down on the tap-dancer's floor,
The sorrow and pain of our mutable status,
With neurons ablaze, a shower of sparks,
All the songs in our heads, the fallen rose petals,
A plunge, applause, a reprieve on the face of it,
They leave you and leave you with only desire,
Condemned to maturity and a sure sense of style.

SUMMER ON REWIND

Julie Bruck

A man and a woman walk backwards
from opposite directions, turn and meet
on a corner, while emergency vehicles scream
across 34ᵗʰ Street, against the one-way signs.
Their embrace lasts so long the homeless
back off, withdraw their cracked palms.
A small car takes them up the Thruway,
trunk-first. Although she appears
to be driving, both stare at the receding
skyline like riders in a caboose.
They shimmy from the car, lunch hurtles
from their mouths, rearranges itself
on plates; wine flows into a bottle,
sealed with original cork, metal closure.
A waitress takes everything away.
In the middle of a lake, they tread water,
laughing and kissing, lips losing their blue.
They swim in feet-first on their stomachs;
toes begin a perfect arc and they're upright
on the dock, towels reattached to dry bodies.
Sleep ends in exhaustion, figures weaving
on a narrow bed; buttons are fastened
with pleasure. They're bright-eyed, shot
through with energy as a second man stands
between them holding a drink, indicating
one to the other. Each withdraws a hand,
each toddles backwards. She goes to her
parked car, repacks a suitcase. A friend's
sedan swallows him, backs down the road.
It is morning. It is night. It is the day
before and the lake is a pane of glass.
Then, a small disturbance by the dock:

a circle of ripples contracts, as a hawk
drops its small fish and travels tail-first,
up into the clear blue on a backwards path
so clean, so purposeful it seems each talon,
each muscle, each fragile bone wants
nothing but to hunger, higher, alone.

AFTER LIFE

Ruth Roach Pierson

Volker brought a bottle of Slivovitz and a new girlfriend named
Veronica. After dinner, I proposed we all play poker. You became
upset when I started introducing one variation after another, and
I grew angry with your impatience. I should have stopped with the
basics, the hierarchy of winning hands—one pair, two pair, three
of a kind, etc. I should never have moved on to seven card stud,
the use of wild cards—Jokers, deuces, one-eyed Jacks. Although
I don't ordinarily drink hard liquor, the Slivovitz, smooth and
viscous with a trace of plum, went down easy. We had polished
off the bottle by midnight, and by then a giant moon had hijacked
the sky. You and I (Volker and Veronica had by this time slipped
away) stepped out of the cottage into a silver-screen world, the
night air lit as though with a zillion fireflies. We made our way
toward the lake through a low-hanging mist glittering with
lunar dust until, transfigured, we became part of that shimmer.
Casting my mind back to that night, I'm reminded of *After Life*,
the Japanese movie that asks what moment from your life you
would choose to live in for all eternity. And I think, well, maybe
that one—that moment of transport we wordlessly shared as we
walked down to the lake, tipsy with Slivovitz, agog at the gauzy,
moon-glistening world, your impatience and my anger folding like
a losing poker hand and disappearing beneath the lake's sparkling
surface. Yes, it will do.

Hope You

Margaret Christakos

enjoyed *8 Mile* I'm going to see *Roger
Dodger* ASAP thinking it might illuminate you a
little to me Almost saw it in NY
on Saturday but went to a cool extremely

minimalist electronic music show instead The main performer
wired a mixing board to send output back
through channels producing feedback of almost unbearable if
a little melodic high frequencies Another player rubbed

a reed up and down over a drumhead
and the quivering vibrations produced static which served
as a low dodge-and-burn intensifier In a dumpy
cement gallery space on the Lower East Side

about fifty very cool young people plus me
sat in reverent silence just a few of
them pressing fingers in their ears to protect
themselves I thought the whole thing would have

been better on drugs but even still it
sent up a blooming whining metaphor of how
my psyche has singed and squealed yet made
no sound at all waiting and feeling the

outer limits these past several months Rather simultaneously
exciting and too mundane for language's access Anyway
New York is a place where art is
Relevant and I think I'd like to live

There The rather preposterously empathetic roster of papers
given on Acker at the symposium I attended
made anyone think it's a good idea to
die young if you're gonna write I don't

know why I'm writing you today just because
I think it's very grey and fallish outside
Like dusk like the busride melancholy fills the
Body and language spills into space like a

Secret shimmer Why feel anything but sometimes the
thing itself feels its way beyond the body
like a semaphore from a border an empire
of the senseful and I become a secretary

Another movie that brought you to mind Ah
cinema, popcorn—

ACKNOWLEDGEMENTS AND PERMISSIONS

Reprinted with acknowledgement of the author
and permission of the publisher.

"Stillness" from Maleea Acker's *The Reflecting Pool* (Pedlar Press, 2009).

"Belle de Jour" from Rishma Dunlop's *Lover Through Departure: New and Selected Poems* (Mansfield Press, 2011), originally published in *White Album* (Inanna Publications, 2008).

"Short Fat Flicks," from Don McKay's *Camber: Selected Poems 1983-2000* (McClelland & Stewart, 2004), originally published in *Apparatus* (McClelland & Stewart, 1997).

"On s'est perdus de vue" from George Sipos' *The Glassblowers* (Goose Lane Editions, 2010).

"Late Movies with Skyler" from Michael Ondaatje, *The Cinnamon Peeler: Selected Poems* (McClelland & Stewart, 1989). Permission of the author.

"After the Movies with O." from John Barton's *Designs from the Interior* (Anansi, 1994).

"Cinema Paradiso" from Jennica Harper's *The Octopus and Other Poems* (Signature Editions, 2006).

"On Watching an Eastern Bloc Comedy" by Rebecca Păpucaru from *Existere: A Journal of Art & Literature* (Spring/Summer 2009).

"*2001,* An Elegy" from Steven Heighton's *The Address Book* (House of Anansi Press, 2004).

"Best in Show" by Sharon McCartney from *Hard Ass* (Palimpsest Press, 2013), first appeared in *The Malahat Review,* No. 176 (September 2011).

"Movies" from George Whipple's *Collage* (Ekstasis Editions, 2012).

"Echoes—A Glosa" from Kildare Dobbs' *Casablanca: the Poem* (Ekstasis Editions, 1999).

"Disgraceland" from Jim Johnstone's *Patternicity* (Nightwood Editions, 2010).

"Resume Drowning" from Darren Bifford's *Wedding in Fire Country* (Nightwood Editions, 2012).

"Ivan's Birches" from Barry Dempster's *Ivan's Birches* (Pedlar Press, 2009).

"On the Day We Were Married" from Elizabeth Bachinsky's *god of missed connections* (Nightwood Editions, 2009).

"A Procession of Travelers" from Lillian Necakov's *Polaroids* (Coach House Books, 1997).

"Eric Rohmer's *Summer*" from Carole Glasser Langille's *Late in a Slow Time* (Mansfield Press, 2003).

"The Emperor, Now a Citizen, Digs His First Hole" from Robert Colman's *Little Empires* (Quattro Books, 2012).

"Glenn Gould Watches *Thirty-Two Short Films about Glenn Gould*" from Steve McOrmond's *Lean Days* (Wolsak and Wynn, 2004).

"La Grosse Maudite Anglaise" from Carolyn Marie Souaid's *October* (Nuage Editions, 1999).

"On Once Again Watching Bruce McDonald's *Hard Core Logo*" from Carleton Wilson's *The Material Sublime* (Nightwood Editions, 2011).

"Jack Dawson's Grave" from Jeanette Lynes' *A Woman Alone on the Atikokan Highway* (Wolsak and Wynn, 1999).

"Upon First Looking through a Rubber Mask into Lynch's *Mulholland Dr.*" by Daniel Scott Tysdal previously appeared in the *Windsor Review* (2006) and *The Rusty Toque* (2013).

"Clarissa's Return" by Kurt Zubatiuk previously published in *Opus III, A Conspiracy in XV Variations* (Aeolus House, 2008).

"Sergeant Brown" from Emily Schultz's *songs for the dancing chicken* (ECW Press, 2007).

"Elle Lolls at Her Pool" by Molly Peacock appeared as "Elle Supine at Her Pool" in *Poetry International*, Vol. 17, 2011, and a prose version will appear in *AlphabeTique: the Lives of the Letters* (McClelland and Stewart).

"Listening to a Recently Dried-Out Lena While Watching Harold Lloyd Hang from a Clock Face at The Mayfair" from Peter Richardson's *Bit Parts for Fools* (Goose Lane Editions, 2013).

"The Day Fatty Arbuckle Died: June 29, 1933 (Clyde Barrow mourns the loss of a possible pal)" by Carolyn Smart first appeared in *Prism International* (Winter 2012).

Brian Bartlett's "From *Being Charlie*" is from *Being Charlie* (The Alfred Gustav Press, 2009).

"After the Chuck Jones Tribute on Teletoon" from Sharon McCartney's *Karenin Sings the Blues* (Goose Lane Editions, 2003), first appeared in the Malahat Review (Fall 2002) and was reprinted in *The Year's Best of Fantasy and Horror*, 16th Annual Edition (St. Martin's Press, 2003).

"Starring Bette Davis" by Jacob Scheier first appeared in *Misunderstandings* 9 (Spring 2008).

"Kirk Douglas Walking along Phipps Street on a Sunny Afternoon" from David W. McFadden's *What's the Score? 99 Poems* (Mansfield Press, 2012).

"Love Poem for a Private Dick" from Karen Solie's *Short Haul Engine* (Brick Books, 2001).

"Samurai" from Michael Kenyon's *The Sutler* (Brick Books, 2005).

"Longshoreman" by Mark Callanan first appeared in *The Newfoundland Quarterly* (Fall 2010).

"Happy Birthday Mr. President, May 1962" from Marilyn Bowering's *Human Bodies: New and Collected Poems 1987-1999* (Porcepic Books, an imprint of Beach Holme Publishing, 1999, with permission from Dundurn Press Ltd).

"The Death of Marilyn Monroe" from Sharon Olds' *The Dead and the Living*, © 1987, reprinted by permission of Alfred A. Knopf, a division of Random House, Inc.

"The Tool Shed Bar, East Sunny Dunes" from RM Vaughan's *ruined stars* (ECW Press, 2004).

"Stunt" from Adam Sol's *Crowd of Sounds* (House of Anansi Press, 2003).

"The Photo Double" from David Seymour's *For Display Purposes Only* (Coach House Books, 2013), first appeared in *The Best of Canadian Poetry in English 2010*, ed. by Lorna Crozier, series editor Molly Peacock (Tightrope Books, 2010).

"The Buried" from Catherine Graham's *Winterkill* (Insomniac Press, 2010).

"Cameo Appearance" from Charles Simic's *The Voice at 3:00 A.M.* (Harcourt, 2003), first published in *Walking the Black Cat* (Mariner Books, 1996), reprinted with permission of the author.

"Sight and Sound" from Todd Swift's *Rue du Regard* (DC Books, 2004), © Todd Swift.

"Hearing Pan" by Craig Poile, first appeared in *The Malahat Review* (Summer 2006), republished in *Seminal: The Anthology of Canadian Gay Male Poetry*, ed. by John Barton and Billeh Nickerson (Arsenal Pulp Press, 2007) and *True Concessions* (Goose Lane Editions, 2009).

"His Domestic Pleasures Song" from Ken Babstock's *Days into Flatspin* (House of Anansi, 2001).

"Geraldine" from David Donnell's *Watermelon Kindness* (ECW Press, 2010).

"Cukaloris" from Jason Guriel's *Pure Products* (Signal Editions, 2009).

"Claude Jutra's Note" by gillian harding-russell first appeared in *The Capilano Review*, No. 43 (1987).

"Souvenir" by Jeramy Dodds first appeared in *The Walrus*, Spring 2013.

"Excerpts from the Future Memoirs of Roger Ebert" by Jacob McArthur Mooney first appeared in *The Windsor Review* (Spring 2013).

"Werewolf Movies" from Margaret Atwood's *Selected Poems II: Poems Selected & New 1976-1986* (Oxford University Press, Canada, 1986).

"*Bride of Frankenstein*" from Alex Boyd's *Making Bones Walk* (Luna Publications, 2007). © Alex Boyd.

"King Kong Meets Wallace Stevens" from Michael Ondaatje's *The Cinnamon Peeler: Selected Poems* (McClelland & Stewart, Inc., 1989). Permission of the author.

"Monster (Godzilla)" from Sachiko Murakami's *The Invisibility Exhibit* (Talon Books, 2008).

"Film Noir" from Carmine Starnino's *This Way Out* (Gaspereau Press, 2009), p. 44.

"Scary Movies" from Kim Addonizio's *What is This Thing Called Love* (W.W. Norton, 2004), permission of the author.

"Movie Monster" from Blaise Moritz' *Zeppelin* (Nightwood Editions, 2013).

"Screenplay by King" from Dave Margoshes' *The Horse Knows the Way* (BuschekBooks, 2009).

"New Rats" from Emily Schultz's *songs for the dancing chicken* (Toronto: ECW Press, 2007).

"James Bond Considers Retirement" by Paula Jane Remlinger first appeared in *Spring* (Saskatchewan Writers' Guild), Vol. 5, Fall 2007.

"Frontier, in Cinecolor" by George Amabile first appeared in *Carte Blanche*, issue 7, of the online literary review of the Quebec Writers' Federation.

"Slow Motion" from Lillian Necakov's *Polaroids* (Coach House Books, 1997).

"Article of Faith" from Adam Sol's *Jonah's Promise* (Mid-List Press, 2000).

"Depression Pictures" from Glen Downie's *An X-Ray of Longing* (Polestar Press, 1987).

"Film in an Unknown Tongue" from A.F. Moritz's *Early Poems* (Insomniac Press, 2002).

"Oz: A Tribute to Gerda Taro" from John Reibetanz's *Afloat* (Brick Books, 2013).

"Emerald City Blues" from Phoebe Tsang's *Contents of a Mermaid's Purse* (Tightrope Books, 2009).

"Instruments from Oz or Paranoid Indian" from David Groulx's *A Difficult Beauty* (Wolsak & Wynn, 2011).

"John" from Jim Smith's *Back Off, Assassin! New and Selected Poems* (Mansfield Press, 2009).

"*Apocalypse Now*" from Patrick Warner's *All manner of misunderstanding* (Killick Press, 2001).

"What we remember" by Jim Nason, an earlier draft of which appeared in *Diving Divas: 100 Gay Men On Their Muses*, ed. by Michael Montlack (Lethe Press, New Jersey, 2012).

"The woman in the carpet" from Maxianne Berger's *Dismantled Secrets* (Wolsak and Wynn, 2008) first appeared in *The North American Review* (January/February 2001) and was republished facing its translation into French by Jean-Pierre Pelletier in *Brèves littéraires* (March 2010).

"Open" from Lorri Neilsen Glenn's *Combustion* (Brick Books, 2007).

"Stormblue" from Robyn Sarah's *Questions About the Stars* (Brick Books, 1998, reprinted by Brick Books in 2012), anthologized in Brick Books' 25-year anthology *New Life in Dark Seas* (Brick Books, 2000), ed. by Stan Dragland, © Robyn Sarah.

"Fargo in Flood," © Stephanie Bolster from *Two Bowls of Milk* (McClelland & Stewart, 1999).

"In Memoriam Stan Brakhage (1933-2003)" from Phil Hall's *An Oak Hunch* (Brick Books, 2005).

"How can you fall asleep?" from "August after August: 6. Iron" in Tonja Gunvaldsen Klaassen's *Lean-to* (Gaspereau Press, 2009).

"Summer on Rewind" from Julie Bruck's *The Woman Downstairs* (Brick Books, 1993).

"After Life" from Ruth Roach Pierson's *Contrary* (Tightrope Books, 2011).

"Hope You" from Margaret Christakos' *What Stirs* (Coach House Books, 2008).

"Hiroshima. Mon amour" from Colin Morton's *Winds and Strings* (BuschekBooks, 2013).

CONTRIBUTORS

Maleea Acker is the author of *The Reflecting Pool, Air-Proof Green* (Pedlar, 2009 & 2013) and *Gardens Aflame: Garry Oak Meadows of BC's South Coast* (New Star, 2012).

Kim Addonizio lives in Oakland, California. She is the author of five poetry collections, two novels, and two story collections. Visit her online at www.kimaddonizio.com.

George Amabile has published ten books and has had work in dozens of the most prestigious journals and anthologies in the English-speaking world.

Margaret Atwood—poet, novelist, literary critic, essayist, and environmentalist—has published over 50 books and won more than 55 awards in Canada and internationally.

Ken Babstock lives in Toronto and won the 2012 Griffin Poetry Prize for *Methodist Hatchet* (House of Anansi, 2011).

Elizabeth Bachinsky is the author of five books of poetry, most recently *The Hottest Summer in Recorded History* (Nightwood, 2013). She lives in Vancouver, BC.

Brian Bartlett is the author of six collections and five chapbooks of poetry, including *The Watchmaker's Table*, *Wanting the Day: Selected Poems*, and *The Afterlife of Trees*.

John Barton's eleven books of poems include *For the Boy with the Eyes of the Virgin: Selected Poems* (Nightwood, 2012), and *Polari* (Gooselane, 2014). He edits *The Malahat Review* in Victoria.

Maxianne Berger is a poet and literary translator. She is active in both the English and French haiku and tanka communities. She lives in Montreal.

Darren Bifford is the author of *Wedding in Fire Country* (Nightwood Editions, 2012). He currently lives in Montreal.

Governor General's Award-winning poet Stephanie Bolster has published four collections of poetry and edited two anthologies. She teaches creative writing at Concordia University in Montreal.

Jacqueline Bourque grew up along the ocean shores of New Brunswick. She is currently at work on her first collection of poetry.

Marilyn Bowering is a poet and novelist who lives in Sooke, B.C. She is the librettist of 'Marilyn Forever', with music by Gavin Bryars. www.marilybowering.com

Alex Boyd is the author of *Making Bones Walk* (2007), winner of the Gerald Lampert Memorial Award, and *The Least Important Man* (2012).

Julie Bruck lives in San Francisco. Her most recent book is *Monkey Ranch*, which won the 2012 Governor General's Literary Award for Poetry.

Mark Callanan was born and raised in St. John's, Newfoundland. *Gift Horse*, his second poetry collection, was shortlisted for the BMO Winterset Award.

Weyman Chan lives and plays in Calgary. His second book of poetry, *Noise From the Laundry*, was finalist for the 2008 Governor General's Award.

Sue Chenette, a classical pianist as well as a poet, is an editor for Brick Books and the author of *Slender Human Weight* and *The Bones of His Being*, both from Guernica Editions.

Margaret Christakos is a Canadian poet who has published nine collections of poetry and a novel. Since 2006 she has facilitated Influency: A Toronto Poetry Salon.

David Clink has two collections of serious poetry, *Eating Fruit Out of Season* and *Monster*, and one collection of humorous verse, *Crouching Yak, Hidden Emu*.

Robert Colman is a Newmarket, Ont.-based writer and editor. His second collection of poems, *Little Empires*, was published by Quattro Books in October 2012.

Barry Dempster, twice nominated for the Governor General's Award, is the author of fourteen poetry collections. He won the Canadian Authors' Association Award for poetry in 2005.

Kildare Dobbs, born Irish in India, was awarded the *Order of Ontario* in 2002 and the *Order of Canada* in 2013. His first of 18 books won a Governor General's Award. *The Kindly Fruits* (2013) is his last.

Jeramy Dodds' first collection, *Crabwise to the Hounds* (Coach House Books, 2008), won the Trillium Book Award for poetry and was shortlisted for the Griffin Poetry Prize.

David Donnell's books of poetry include *Settlements*, winner of the Governor General's Award, *China Blues*, winner of the City of Toronto Book Award, and most recently *Watermelon Kindness*.

Glen Downie has published film reviews and several poetry collections including the recent *Left for Right*. His *Loyalty Management* won a Toronto Book Award.

Rishma Dunlop is the author of five books of poetry: *Lover Through Departure, White Album, Metropolis, Reading Like a Girl,* and *The Body of My Garden*.

Eric Folsom is the author of *Icon Driven* and *Northeastern Anti-Ghazals* among other collections. He is currently the Poet Laureate of Kingston, Ontario.

Michael Fraser has published both nationally and internationally in various anthologies and journals. His first collection, *The Serenity of Stone*, was published by Bookland Press.

Lorri Neilsen Glenn is the author and editor of thirteen collections of poetry and prose, including *Threading Light: Explorations in Loss and Poetry* (Hagios 2011) and *Untying the Apron: Daughters Remember Mothers of the 1950s* (Guernica Editions, 2013) now in its third printing.

Catherine Graham is the author of five poetry collections. She teaches Creative Writing at the University of Toronto School of Continuing Studies. Visit: www.catherinegraham.com

Marlene Grand Maitre's poetry has been published in anthologies and literary journals. One of her poems was longlisted for *Best Canadian Poetry In English* 2011.

Elizabeth Greene has published two collections of poetry, *The Iron Shoes* and *Moving*. Her new book *Understories* is scheduled to appear from Inanna in 2014.

David Groulx's poetry has appeared in over 160 publications in 16 countries. His 6th collection of poems, *Imagine Mercy*, appeared in 2013.

Jason Guriel's work has appeared in *Poetry, The Walrus, Parnassus, PN Review*. His latest book: *The Pigheaded Soul: Essays and Reviews on Poetry and Culture* (Porcupine's Quill, 2013).

Phil Hall's *Killdeer* (2011) won the Governor General's Award for Poetry as well as Ontario's Trillium Award. His most recent book is *The Small Nouns Crying Faith* (2013). He lives near Perth, Ontario.

gillian harding-russell's poems have most recently come out in the anthologies *That Not Forgotten* (Hidden Brook Press) and *Poet to Poet* (Guernica, 2012).

Jennica Harper's books are *What It Feels Like for a Girl* (Anvil Press, 2008) and *The Octopus and Other Poems* (Signature Editions, 2006).

Maureen Scott Harris' collections of poems are: *A Possible Landscape* (Brick), *Drowning Lessons* (Pedlar, 2005 Trillium Book Award for Poetry), and *Slow Curve Out* (Pedlar).

Steven Heighton has published 12 books of poetry, fiction, and essays. His work has appeared in *Poetry, Best American Poetry, LRB, TLR,* and the *NYTBR.* A GG Award finalist for poetry, he has won four gold National Magazine awards.

Louisa Howerow's poetry has appeared in anthologies, journals and small print magazines in Canada, Australia, and the United States.

Maureen Hynes has published three books of poetry, *Harm's Way* (for which she won the Gerald Lampert award), *Rough Skin,* and *Marrow, Willow.* www.maureenhynes.ca

Jim Johnstone is the author of four books of poetry, including *Dog Ear* (Véhicule Press, 2014) and *Patternicity* (Nightwood Editions, 2010), and a past winner of the CBC Poetry Prize.

Donna Kane is the author of two books of poetry, and her writing has appeared in anthologies, journals and magazines across Canada.

Michael Kenyon is the author of fourteen books. Latest is the novel, *A Year at River Mountain.* He lives on the West Coast.

Raised in Saskatchewan when Saskatoon's Capitol Theatre was torn down, Tonja Gunvaldsen Klaassen frequented the repertory Broadway Theatre in Saskatoon, and now lives near The Oxford in Halifax.

Carole Glasser Langille's fourth book of poems, *Church of the Exquisite Panic: The Ophelia Poems,* published in the fall of 2012, was shortlisted for The Atlantic Poetry Prize..

Mat Laporte is a student. In his spare time he makes small press chapbooks with the publishing collective Ferno House. He lives in Toronto.

Multi-genre writer Shelley A. Leedahl's latest books are *Listen, Honey* (stories, DC Books) and *Wretched Beast* (poetry, BuschekBooks). She lives in Edmonton, hails from Saskatchewan.

Ian LeTourneau is the author of *Defining Range* (Gaspereau, 2006) and *Terminal Moraine* (Thistledown, 2008). He's poetry co-editor of *The Fiddlehead*. He lives in Fredericton.

Jeanette Lynes' *Archive of the Undressed* (2012) is her sixth poetry collection. She is Coordinator of the MFA in Writing at the University of Saskatchewan.

Tanis MacDonald is the author of three books of poetry, most recently *Rue the Day*. She teaches at Wilfrid Laurier University in Waterloo.

Kirsteen MacLeod's poetry and prose has appeared in *CV2, TNQ* and *The Malahat Review*. She adores being 'alone in the dark'— especially at a film.

Nathan Mader lives and writes in his hometown of Regina. In 2002, he graduated from Victoria Motion Picture School and spent a number of years working on Vancouver Island.

Saskatoon-area writer Dave Margoshes' most recent poetry collection, *Dimensions of an Orchard,* won the Anne Szumigalski Poetry Prize at the 2010 Saskatchewan Book Awards.

Sharon McCartney has published four collections of poetry. She received the Acorn/Plantos People's Poetry Prize for *The Love Song of Laura Ingalls Wilder* (Nightwood Editions, 2007). Her latest is *Hard Ass* (Palimpsest Press 2013).

David W. McFadden is the author of thirty-five books of poetry, fiction and travel writing. He is the recipient of the 2013 Griffin Prize for Poetry.

Don McKay, awarded the GG for Poetry twice and the Griffin Poetry Prize in 2007, most recently published *Paradoxides* (poems) and *The Shell of the Tortoise* (essays). He resides in St. John's.

rob mclennan is the author of more than two dozen books of poetry, fiction and non-fiction in five countries. Find him at robmclennan. blogspot.com

Steve McOrmond is the author of three collections of poetry, most recently *The Good News about Armageddon* (Brick Books 2010). He lives in Toronto.

Kelsey J. Mills is a writer, avid comic book fan and a movie lover. Her favourite movie is *Looper*, but that is always subject to change.

Vanessa Moeller's poems and short stories have appeared in numerous periodicals. Her first poetry collection, *Our Extraordinary Monsters,* was published by Signature Editions in 2009.

Jacob McArthur Mooney's favourite films are *King Kong* and *Quiz Show*. He's the author of *The New Layman's Almanac* (McClelland & Stewart, 2008) and *Folk* (M&S, 2011).

A.F. Moritz's most recent book of poems is *The New Measures*. For three years he wrote a weekly film column for the Milwaukee *Sentinel* and for twelve years taught a film course at St. Michael's College, U of T.

Blaise Moritz lives in East Toronto. He is the author of *Zeppelin* (Nightwood Editions, 2013) and *Crown and Ribs* (Fitzhenry and Whiteside, 2007). blaisemoritz.com

Ottawa writer Colin Morton has published a novel, *Oceans Apart,* and ten books of poetry, most recently *Winds and Strings* (BuschekBooks, 2013) and *The Hundred Cuts.*

Sachiko Murakami is the author of the poetry collections *The Invisibility Exhibit* (Talonbooks, 2008), a finalist for the Governor General's Literary Award and the Gerald Lampert Memorial Award, and *Rebuild* (Talonbooks, 2011).

Jim Nason is the author of four collections of poetry, a collection of short stories and two novels. Originally from Montreal, he presently lives in Toronto.

Lillian Necakov is the author of *Sickbed of Dogs, Polaroids, Hat Trick, The Bone Broker,* and *Hooligans.* She runs the Boneshaker Reading Series.

Sharon Olds has published 12 collections of poetry, most recently *Stag's Leap* (Knopf, 2012) which won the T.S. Eliot Prize.

Michael Oliver resides in Charlottetown, Prince Edward Island, and has published poetry in many places. His most recent book is a novella called *The Final Cause of Love.*

Winner of the GG for *The Collected Works of Billy the Kid, Running in the Family,* and *The English Patient* (also awarded the Man Booker Prize), Michael Ondaatje is the author of 13 books of poetry.

Shortlisted for *Arc's* Poem of the Year, Rebecca Păpucaru's work has appeared in *Prism International, The Antigonish Review,* and *The Best Canadian Poetry in English.*

Mitchell Parry has published two books of poetry, both with Goose Lane Editions. He teaches Film Studies at the University of Victoria.

Lisa Pasold grew up in Montreal which gave her the jaywalking skills to survive as a journalist. Her latest book, *Any Bright Horse,* was nominated for a Governor General's Award.

Widely anthologized writer Molly Peacock is the author of *The Paper Garden: Mrs. Delany Begins Her Life's Work at 72* and *The Second Blush,* poems.

Ruth Roach Pierson, author of *Where No Window Was,* GG finalist *Aide-Mémoire,* and *CONTRARY,* has attended TIFF since 1980, 33 films in 10 days her personal best.

Craig Poile lives in Ottawa. He recently revisited childhood thrills by watching *The Muppet Movie* and *Superman 2* with his daughters Lily and Samantha.

Claudia Coutu Radmore is author of *a minute or two/ without remembering*, 2010, and *Accidentals*, (Apt. 9 Press, Ottawa), the 2011 bpNichols Chapbook Award winner.

John Reibetanz's eighth collection of poems, *Afloat*, was published by Brick Books in 2013. He lives in Toronto and teaches English and creative writing at Victoria College.

Paula Jane Remlinger lives in Beaver Creek, SK. Her poetry has appeared in *Grain*, *TNQ*, and other journals. She loves to watch terrible movies.

Peter Richardson's most recent poetry collections are: *Sympathy for the Couriers* (Véhicule Press, 2007) and *Bit Parts for Fools* (Goose Lane Editions, 2013).

Patria Rivera's first collection, *Puti/White*, was shortlisted for Trillium Book Award for Poetry in 2006. She's also won the Filipino Global Literary Award for Poetry.

Freelance writer Patricia Dawn Robertson lives in Wakaw, Saskatchewan with fellow writer, D. Grant Black. She has published one poetry chapbook, *Seven Year Itch*.

Julie Roorda is the author of three volumes of poetry, and a collection of short stories, all published by Guernica, as well as a novel for young adults. She lives in Toronto.

Elizabeth Ross teaches, edits, and writes in Toronto. Her first book is forthcoming with Palimpsest Press.

Jeffrey Round is a writer and filmmaker. His latest book is the noir-thriller, *Lake On The Mountain*, a 2013 Lambda Award winner. Visit his website: www.jeffreyround.com.

Robyn Sarah has published nine poetry collections, two story collections and a book of essays on poetry. Her poems have been anthologized in Canada, the US and the UK.

Jacob Scheier is the author of two poetry collections, including the Governor General's Award winning *More to Keep us Warm* (ECW Press, 2007).

Eleonore Schönmaier is the author of *Wavelengths of Your Song* and *Treading Fast Rivers*. Her award winning writing has been published and translated internationally.

Emily Schultz is the co-founder of *Joyland Magazine*. Her books include the novel *The Blondes* and the collection *Songs for the Dancing Chicken*, which was a Trillium Poetry Award finalist.

Winnipeg-based poet Brenda Sciberras' work has appeared in Canadian literary journals as well as in anthologies. Her first book of poetry is with Turnstone Press.

David Seymour has published two poetry collections: *Inter Alia* (Brick Books, 2005) and *For Display Purposes Only* (Coach House, 2013). David works as an assistant director in the film industry in Toronto.

Serbian-American Charles Simic served as co-poetry editor of the *Paris Review*, 15th Poet Laureate of in the USA, and won the Pulitzer Prize for Poetry in 1990.

George Sipos lives on Salt Spring Isl... ...s third book, *The Geography of Arrival*, was short-lis... ...for the Charles Taylor Award for Literary Non-Fiction in 2011.

Carolyn Smart is the author of a memoir, *At the End of the Day*, and five collections of poetry, most recently *Hooked—Seven Poems* (Brick Books, 2009).

Jim Smith's *Back Off, Assassin: New and Selected* was long-listed for the 2010 GG's Poetry Award. His *Happy Birthday, Nicanor Parra* (also Mansfield) appeared in 2012.

Adam Sol's most recent collection of poetry *Complicity* was published in spring 2014 by McClelland and Stewart. His previous collections include *Jonah's Promise, Crowd of Sounds* and *Jeremiah, Ohio*.

Karen Solie was born in Moose Jaw and lives in Toronto. *Pigeon* (2009) won the 2010 Griffin Poetry Prize and the Trillium Book Award for Poetry.

Carolyn Marie Souaid has published 7 books of poetry and edited over a dozen. Her videopoem *Blood is Blood* won an award at the 2012 Berlin Zebra Poetry Film Festival.

Carmine Starnino's most recent book of poems, *This Way Out* (Gaspereau, 2009), was nominated for a Governor General's Award. He lives in Montreal.

Sandra Stechisen lives and writes in Winnipeg. Her work has appeared in literary publications such as *CV2* and *Event Magazine*.

The Director of Eyewear Publishing and teacher at Glasgow University, Todd Swift has a PhD from the University of East Anglia (UEA). He has published eight full collections of poetry and edited numerous anthologies.

Christine Joy Tan is a recent University of Toronto Scarborough graduate. She catches matinee movie screenings and eats deliciously greasy foods in and around Toronto.

Richard Teleky, a Professor at York University, has most recently published *The Dog on the Bed*, a study of the human/dog bond, and *The Hermit in Arcadia*, poems.

Souvankham Thammavongsa is the author of three poetry books from Pedlar Press: *Light* (2013), *Found* (2007), and *Small Arguments* (2003). She was educated in Toronto.

Nick Thran is the author of two collections of poems and one book for children. *Earworm* (Nightwood Editions, 2011) won the Trillium Book Award for Poetry.

Poet, librettist and short story writer Phoebe Tsang's poetry collection is *Contents of a Mermaid's Purse* (Tightrope Books). She has lived and travelled throughout Canada.

Deborah-Anne Tunney lives in Ottawa. Her short stories and poetry have been published in Canada, the United States, and the Middle East.

Daniel Scott Tysdal is the award-winning author of two books of poetry. He teaches at the University of Toronto Scarborough.

RM Vaughan is a Toronto-based writer and video artist. Please visit www.rmvaughan.ca

Patrick Warner has published four collections of poetry, most recently *Perfection* (Goose Lane/Ice House, 2012). He is twice winner of the E.J. Pratt Poetry Prize.

Born 1927 in St. John's, Newfoundland, George Whipple is the author of 15 books of poetry. A resident of Toronto for 50 years, he now lives in Burnaby, B.C.

Carleton Wilson is a poet and book designer. His book, *The Material Sublime*, was published in 2011 by Nightwood Editions. He lives in Toronto.

Patricia Young has published eleven collections of poetry and one of short fiction. She lives in Victoria, BC.

Kurt Zubatiuk is a poet and psychotherapist. His poetry collection, *Ekstasis,* was published by LYRICALMYRICAL Press in 2007. He lives in Toronto.

List of Movies Referenced

2001: A Space Odyssey, USA, 1968, dir. Stanley Kubrick.

8 Mile, USA, 2002, dir. Curtis Hanson.

Abbott and Costello Meet Frankenstein (Dracula and the Wolf Man), USA, 1948, dir. Charles Barton.

After Life, Japan, 1998, dir. Hirokazu Kore-eda.

Amarcord, Italy, 1973, dir. Federico Fellini.

Apocalypse Now, USA, 1979, dir. Francis Ford Coppola.

Back to the Future, USA, 1985, dir. Robert Zemeckis.

Being John Malkovich, USA, 1999, dir. Spike Jonze

Belle de Jour, France, 1967, dir. Luis Buñuel.

Ben-Hur, USA, 1959, dir. William Wyler.

Best in Show, USA, 2000, dir. Christopher Guest.

Bicycle Thieves, Italy, 1948, dir. Vittorio De Sica.

Breathless (À bout de souffle), France, 1960, dir. Jean-Luc Godard.

Bride of Frankenstein, USA, 1935, dir. James Whale.

Casablanca, USA, 1942, dir. Michael Curtiz.

Cinema Paradiso, Italy, 1988, dir. Giuseppe Tornatore.

Days of Heaven, USA, 1978, dir. Terrence Malick.

Earth (Zemlya), USSR, 1930, dir. Aleksandr Dovzhenko (Ukrainian).

Elevator to the Gallows (Ascenseur poul l'échafand), France, 1957, dir. Louis Malle.

Fargo, USA, 1986, dir. Joel and Ethan Coen.

Film, USA, 1965, dir. Alan Schneider, script Samuel Beckett.

Fly Away Baby, USA, 1937, dir. Frank McDonald.

Funny Face, USA, 1957, dir. Stanley Donen.

Gabbeh, Iran, 1996, dir. Mohsen Makmalbaf.

Giant, USA, 1956, dir. George Stevens.

Godzilla, Japan, 1954, dir. Ishirō Honda.

Grizzly Man, USA, 2005, dir. Werner Herzog.

Hard Core Logo, Canada, 1996, dir. Bruce McDonald.

Hiroshima mon amour, France, 1959, dir. Alain Renais.

Iris, UK/USA, 2001, dir. Richard Eyre.

Ivan's Childhood, USSR, 1962, dir. Andrei Tarkovsky.

Jules et Jim, France, 1962, dir. François Truffaut.

King Kong, USA, 1933, dir. Merian C. Cooper and Ernest B. Schoedsack.

L'Atalante, France, 1934, dir. Jean Vigo.

La poulette grise, Canada, 1947, NFB, dir. Norman McLaren.

La Règle du jeu (The Rules of the Game), France, 1939, dir. Jean Renoir.

Leave Her To Heaven. USA, 1945, dir. John M. Stahl.

Les enfants du paradis, France, 1945, dir. Marcel Carné.

Mad Love, USA, 1995, dir. Antonia Bird.

Memento, USA, 2002, dir. Christopher Nolan.

Mon oncle Antoine, Québec, 1971, dir. Claude Jutra.

Mrs. Skeffington, USA, 1944, dir. Vincent Sherman.

Mulholland Drive, USA, 2001, dir. David Lynch.

National Velvet, USA, 1944, dir. Clarence Brown.

Nights of Cabiria, Italy, 1957, dir. Federico Fellini.

Nosferatu the Vampyre (Nosferatu: Phantom der Nacht), West Germany, 1979, dir. Werner Herzog.

Nosferatu, A Symphony of Horror, Germany, 1922, dir. F.W. Murnau.

Octobre, Québec, 1994, dir. Pierre Faradeau.

On the Beach, USA, 1959, dir. Stanley Kramer.

On the Waterfront, USA, 1954, dir. Elia Kazan.

Rebel Without a Cause, USA, 1955, dir. Nicholas Ray.

Roger Dodger, USA, 2001, dir. Dylan Kidd.

Roma, Italy, 1972, dir. Federico Fellini.

Rupert of Hentzau, USA, 1923, dir. Victor Heerman.

Safety Last!, USA, 1923, dir. Fred C. Newmeyer and Sam Taylor.

Seven Brides for Seven Brothers, USA, 1954, dir. Stanley Donen.

Shadows of Forgotten Ancestors, USSR, 1968, dir. Sergei Parajanov (Ukrainian of Armenian descent).

Some Like It Hot, USA, 1959, dir. Billy Wilder.

Spellbound, USA, 1945, dir. Alfred Hitchcock.

Summer (Le rayon vert), France, 1986, dir. Éric Rohmer.

Terminator 2: Judgment Day, USA, 1991, dir. James Cameron.

The 400 Blows (Les quatre cents coups), France, 1959, dir. François Truffaut.

The Best Exotic Marigold Hotel, UK, 2012, dir. John Madden.

The Birds, USA, 1963, dir. Alfred Hitchcock.

The Bridge on the River Kwai, USA, 1957, dir. David Lean.

The Dark Knight, UK/USA, 2008, dir. Christopher Nolan.

The Endurance: Shackleton's Legendary Antarctic Expedition, USA, UK, Germany, Sweden, 2000, dir. George Butler.

The English Patient, USA/UK, 1996, dir. Anthony Minghella.

The Haunting, UK, 1963, dir. Robert Wise.

The Hours, UK, USA, 2002/03, dir. Stephen Daldry.

The Last Emperor, Italy, 1987, dir. Bernardo Bertolucci.

The Magician, Sweden, 1958, dir. Ingmar Bergman.

The Prisoner of Zenda, USA, 1937, dir. John Cromwell.

The Rocky Horror Picture Show, USA, 1975, dir. Jim Sharman.

The Seventh Seal, Sweden, 1957, dir. Ingmar Bergman.

The Son of Kong, USA, 1933, dir. Ernest B. Schoedsack.

The Third Man, USA, 1949, dir. Carol Reed.

The Titanic, USA, 1997, dir. James Cameron.

The Wizard of Oz, USA, 1939, dir. Victor Fleming, King Vidor, Mervyn LeRoy.

Thirty-Two Short Films about Glenn Gould, Canada, 1993, dir. François Girard.

Total Recall, USA, 1990, dir. Paul Verhoeven.

Toto le héros, Belgium, 1991, dir. Jaco van Dormael.

Welcome to L.A., USA, 1976, dir. Alan Rudolph.

Whatever Happened to Baby Jane?, USA, 1962, dir. Robert Aldrich.

Zéro de conduite, France, 1933, dir. Jean Vigo.

THANK YOU'S

First and foremost thanks are owing to Sue MacLeod for suggesting this anthology and for her hard work during the initial round of poem selection. Next come the many friends, advisers, readers, and enthusiasts in whose debt I stand for the help they offered, but whose large number prevents me from mentioning more than a few by name. A definite thank you is owed to the first poets I contacted for permission to cite their poems in the project proposal: Barry Dempster, David Donnell (who came up with the book's title), David Seymour, Karen Solie, and Carmine Starnino (who referred me to *The Faber Book of Movie Verse* from 1993). Early on Brian Bartlett drew on his encyclopaedic knowledge of Canadian poetry to recommend titles of movie poems and the names of their poet authors, many now included between the covers of this book. Throughout the sometimes daunting process, I have received consolation and support from friends and colleagues, including Agnes Cserati, Catherine Graham, Maureen Scott Harris, Maureen Hynes, Leslie Hopkins, Jim Johnstone, Mitchell Parry, Molly Peacock, Patria Rivera, Julie Roorda, and Elaine Whittaker. Still others listened sympathetically to my frequent bewilderment (i.e., over spread sheets) and apprehension (i.e., over the seemingly infinite possibilities for error). The harrowing end stages of proofing could simply not have been accomplished without the iron serenity, expertise and steady eye of Heather Wood. To my partner Dwight Boyd, for his unfailing patience and affirmation, there are not enough thank you's in the world. Finally I am hugely grateful to Michael Mirolla who, when I thought all was lost, came to the rescue with the offer to publish and whose geniality, professionalism, efficiency and imperturbability have made working with him an absolute pleasure.

RECYCLED
Paper made from
recycled material
FSC
www.fsc.org   FSC® C100212

819   I found it at the movies.
.154   Aurora P.L.   JUL14
08   33164005171967
0357
I